# JOAN URE
## FIVE SHORT PLAYS

**SCOTTISH SOCIETY OF PLAYWRIGHTS**
Scottish Play Series
1979

# JOAN URE PLAYS: INTRODUCTION

When Joan Ure died early in 1978, at the height of her powers, the loss to Scottish writing, and especially writing for the stage, was immeasurable — such losses cannot in any case be measured, but in hers it was especially poignant, since she was just beginning to receive some of the recognition long overdue to her talents. But, again as in all such cases, regret for the further fruits they might have borne throws light backwards and turns into its opposite, namely gratitude for what they had already produced.

As a playwright Joan Ure left a large body of work behind, much of it unknown except to a minority of that other, slightly larger minority, the playgoing public. The plays were mostly short, and it may be that they were so because she felt they were more likely to get a showing by making modest demands on theatrical resources, but they concentrated an extraordinary amount of thought, feeling, and imagination into small compass. Concentration was always her aim, achieved by allusion, ellipsis, an uncommon capacity to make her every word work for its living and carry as much meaning as possible, and at the same time to move with natural grace. In a word, she was a poet; but though also a lyric poet, one who fully grasped the fact — indeed with all her instincts — that drama is another mode of poetry.

The five plays presented here are indeed no more than a sample, but they are, one hopes, representative both of her brilliant individuality as a playwright, the skill and imagination with which she used the theatre as means, and of the themes that recur throughout her work. Neither, in truth, is separable from the other. That these pieces have all, as the phrase goes, "something to say" — which they undoubtedly and forcibly have — does not cumber them with the depressing description of plays with a message. The plays themselves are messages, each of a unique kind; for when the bringer of tidings arrives, not bearing some news extraneous to himself, but embodying it in his or her person, then although a generalised truth may be abstracted and repeated, the full import is only, and unrepeatably, in the messenger.

The best example is perhaps The Hard Case, the purport of which — arising out of the Ibrox disaster of 1971 and a view of professional football as part of a more general disaster area in our way of life — is a plea for peace "with greater justice." Something so simple, it seems, no one would disagree with or,

# JOAN URE: FIVE SHORT PLAYS

First Published 1979
by
Scottish Society of Playwrights
Copyright  c  Scottish Society of Playwrights
346 Sauchiehall Street, Glasgow

Printed Litho by
Commercial Management Services,
268 Bath Street,
Glasgow  G2  4JR.

ISBN  0 906799 00 7

This is number

of a limited first edition run of 350

possibly, find interesting. But the play leads us to feel, most acutely, what lies in the hinterland of this unexceptionable aspiration, what the want of peace and justice truly is, and how hard are all cases when they come to the bar of an awakened conscience.

It is not a play of slogans or hi-falutin' language — mostly it is couched in just such words as might be used by the ordinary Glasgow businessman who is accused and accuser, plaintiff and judge. But it brings the large abstractions spoken by public men uncomfortably, though also often hilariously, home.

Three of the plays here are a kind of gloss upon Shakespeare, and it is interesting that Joan Ure, who was both modest and heroically daring in her writing, should have set herself, not to improve on him but to pick up, as it were, some of his odds and ends and see what could be made of them. She had an exceedingly sharp eye for the unconsidered trifles of life and art — which are trifling, sometimes, only because they have been unconsidered.

Seven Characters Out of The Dream are (in my belief, and if one must make such gradations) the most perfect of all Joan Ure's works for the stage, and one which exhibits most completely her subtlety, her wit, her marvellous fun, and her real seriousness. In it seven "characters" from A Midsummer Night's Dream, or persons who have assumed their left-over costumes, explore through the seemingly vacuous exchanges of a fancy-dress party the perennial puzzles of Life and Art, appearance and reality; they do it lightly, but with a penetration and conviction of the importance of the task not to be improved on in Pirandello or Ibsen (to name two other writers much taken up with these questions) or, come to that, Shakespeare himself. It is a play, and a very playful one, dedicated to the proposition that art has significance and importance for life, and that one can't get along without the other. At one point a scrap of writing is read out — a good many of Joan Ure's best lines are almost literally thrown away — which may be taken as a quite precise equivalent of the Renaissance artist's aspiration. The writer no longer talks of out-lasting bronze or marble, but is not really aiming lower —

> If I fly, I'll fall
> but it will teach me a little
> how to walk.

Something in it for Cordelia and Something in it for Ophelia could be described as rescue operations for two of the most put-upon of Shakespeare's females. Both have as background productions of the two most famous of the Tragedies at the Edinburgh Festival, and they might be thought of, therefore, as pieces d'occasion. If that is so, each managed triumphantly to rise above its temporal origin. In the first Cordelia, in charge of an ex-King Lear in a wheelchair, traverses the authority of demanding old men, of military tradition (especially the Scottish kind, romantically attached to lost battles and causes) and of self-displaying tragedy itself with a withering fire of good sense and kindness. In the second the position is reversed: the girl who, having just seen a performance of Hamlet, feels that there should be more in it for Ophelia than Shakespeare provided, comes round to acknowledge that, for all practical considerations to the contrary, there is something to be said, if only in mitigation, for the Prince of Denmark.

The play is particularly interesting because Joan Ure, who felt the position of women in society with acute sensibility and sometimes with outrage, is in some danger of being labelled as a "feminist" writer. How far she was from being merely that, and yet how keen an eye she cast upon the variously false "roles" forced on women, and men, by law custom and tradition, can be seen in the last of the plays in this selection. Take Back Your Old Rib, Then is remarkable as much for its honesty about the outrageousness of women on the rampage as for its sympathy, as herself a conscious member, with the currently "emergent nation within the nation." There are passages in it of ironic perception which prompt regret that she did not add, to the all-too obedient and amiable Shakespearean heroines for whom she wrote new parts, some as yet unscheduled scenes for Lady Macbeth.

It should be emphasised again that all these plays, touching — as they do, with conviction, passion, and sharp insight — the sort of issues we call "serious", do so with a continuous play of wit and fun and, often, a truly joyful gaiety. In performance they can frequently be very funny indeed; they are also, as the reader will discover, wonderfully diverting on the page. Joan Ure wrote for performance, as every true playwright must; but it is also true that every play really worth performing — as, most certainly, directors and actors and audiences will increasingly discover hers to be — is worth reading as well.

Promoting both these ends, the publication of texts by the Scottish Society of Playwrights will surely be among its most valuable activities. It is a somewhat bitter thought that Joan Ure, who was a founder-member of the S.S.P. and an unsparing worker on its behalf, should not have lived to see this promising extension of its functions. But there is no question that for the library of contemporary plays by Scottish writers which, it is to be hoped, will be built up under the Society's imprint, her work is the most fitting and vital inauguration.

Christopher Small, Glasgow, April 1979.

# CONTENTS

# LIST OF ILLUSTRATIONS

# SOMETHING IN IT FOR CORDELIA

by

## JOAN URE

## SOMETHING IN IT FOR CORDELIA

is a comedy rescued for Festival 1971 from
Shakespeare and the performance in that
year of KING LEAR at the Assembly Hall.


Characters

**THE OLD LEAR OF SCOTLAND**
**CORDELIA,** his youngest daughter.

Place: Waverley Station, Edinburgh.


Time

The present.
(Just after 10.30 p.m.)

INTRODUCER: A performance of KING LEAR happened in 1971 at the Festival in Edinburgh. It took place in the Assembly Hall. It's due round again pretty soon, but we cannot wait for that. Joan Ure re-typed this play for last year, which was International Woman's Year . . . everywhere but in Scotland that is. But re-typing it made no difference. It still waits for a full production. Just the same the young women nowadays have noticed that there is nothing much for them to do in Shakespeare's plays — Ophelia and Cordelia for instance — except die, rather beautifully. Today it might be different. This play suggests that if King Lear of then had been, instead, King Lear of Scotland now, we might have had not a tragedy which the Scots can't afford but a sort of Steptoe and daughter comedy. The Scots are used to expecting failure, so their King Lear wouldn't have taken it so much to heart. He would just make a quick getaway.
Here we see him, sisters, sitting in a wheelchair, wearing his guilty crown. Waiting in Waverley Station, Edinburgh, for the train. And here is Cordelia in her long court dress, and cycle clips. She has leant her byke against the station wall, while she waits till her father's train to the Highlands comes in. You are to imagine that

Shakespeare's KING LEAR inhabits the Assembly Hall on the Mound, once again, with all the pomp and circumstance that invites. Down here, we need the lights up on the old Lear himself.

LEAR: When there used to be the Old Caledonia Station, even the name gave a man a bit of confidence.

CORDELIA: All trains leave from Waverley now. It sounds more romantic, and it saves expense.

LEAR: It is very confusing. The Old Caledonia had more style.

CORDELIA: Now father, enough of nostalgia. We are well out of that, and you know it. Oil has caught up even with us.

LEAR: Old Caledonia! I can say it and it hardly means a thing — alas.

CORDELIA: That's good then, dear. You will sit in the train facing the way you are going. I'll see that the guard minds your wheelchair. I know you don't really need it but it creates the impression you want.

LEAR: A sort of mobile throne.

CORDELIA: It is that!

LEAR: I know I could depend on Cordelia. A man does not like immediately to lose everything. Her sisters had such simple ideas — Regan and Goneril did — oh they'd have made a success of a term of office. In fact they did. Rule is easy when you don't mind what happens to the kingdom after you've gone. But posterity would have suffered. Cordelia's husband, Donald, and his merry men arrived just in time to save us as a nation.

CORDELIA: We can hope so, father. We can hope. Where will you put the ticket — this bit you submit at Glasgow. This next bit you tender at Oban; after that you are on your own.

LEAR: But I thought you were going on ahead on your bicycle there. To save one fare, and because, as you said, you do not absolutely trust British Railways. Though I cannot see why I could not have been allowed to go by road too. Everybody else does.

CORDELIA: Now remember, your ticket is in your sporran. And your sporran, as usual, is under your cloak.

LEAR: When you get old, people do not always listen when you speak. There are other disadvantages too.

CORDELIA: You go by train, dear, in case it rains. We have only the one raincape between us, and I am not the one who's wearing a crown that tarnishes when it rains.

LEAR: You insisted I dispose of the real gold crown. You said it was our duty to send our family donation to thon famine fund. I think we should have left it to the more affluent monarchies to do that.

CORDELIA: The more affluence, the less charity. Oh father, how do you think folk get rich anyway. They don't get rich by selling their gold crowns and sending the proceeds to charity.

LEAR: Then why insist, as you certainly did? I myself felt that we could not afford it. Even your byke you had to borrow and it's only because of the sheer strength of my character that you allowed me to call my wheelchair my own. You are so hardset against owning property. It means we are living hand to mouth nearly all the time. Some day society may have advanced to the point where people like us can afford to be charitable. But as things are now, we are much better to be rich.

CORDELIA: Father! If mother is listening, you know what she's thinking!

LEAR: Your mother did not expect a person to be just perfect.

CORDELIA: If she had done, she'd have died, not in childbed trying to get you a son, but of a brokenheart and much earlier on.

LEAR: Who are you to decide what your mother died of?

CORDELIA: Dearest father, please don't be contradictory. I know it generates a sort of spontaneous combustion and that makes time pass, if not pleasantly then at least fast. And I know we missed the 10.30 train by a wheel's breadth, although no-one could have come quicker down that Mound than I did, pushing you, while you carried the byke. So we have a good 20 minutes before the next and the last train out of Edinburgh tonight. But I will not argue just for argument's sake.

LEAR: I wish I had my wee fool here now.

CORDELIA: We could not afford the extra half fare. And a wee fool is not really at home in the country. His job is to witness for the wilderness in the places of power.

LEAR: I should never have let your mother encourage you to get an education. There is nothing I can say but you'll answer me back. In my father's time that wasn't even possible: the old man would give you the back of his hand quicker than a look at his watch.

CORDELIA: We have made progress father. Time marches on.

LEAR: Oh you think so!

CORDELIA: Now — as if the train were going into the tunnel — our father figure goes into the huff!!

LEAR: I need just the forty winks. It's been a long day. Already! And we've only just started, as you assure me. I don't know if I wasn't better off with your sisters, Regan and Goneril. All they did was move a few soldiers from one side to the other of the Esplanade.

and that provided at least a spectacle.

CORDELIA: But who encouraged them to put on their show in the Assembly Hall, father? Do you think the Church of Scotland would sanction all that, if they had given it any thought? I know it's supposed to be just a story.

LEAR: Me, just a story!

CORDELIA: But all that tomato ketchup going to waste on the stage while the chips of the poor get served with plain vinegar. Oh father — thrift. Remember — thrift. Waste not while other folk are in want. Who taught me these things? (TO AUDIENCE) My father — the ex-King Lear of Scotland — had a large kingdom once. They have sold its water and turned its lands over to the tourists for deer parks and ski slopes. We make more off the ski slopes than off the deer parks. That is because our winters last longer than other people's. You get folk skooshing down those ski slopes at Aviemore there, patronising our posh hotels and delighting the Italian chef and Scandanavian au pair girls, and it goes well on into what other countries, even in the northern hemisphere, are calling "summer". In the deer parks, there are now very few deer. All gentle creatures get shot down young. It is what is called the slaughter of the innocents. It goes on in this place all the time. People hardly notice it now. Meantime my poor father is having a snooze. Would you guess he was only 55? Well, that's all he is! And Regan and Goneril, my sisters — now deceased — were not 27, not either of them. To survive in this place they realised they had to grow up early on. I was lucky. I escaped. I was banished actually. But I will not reproach my father for that. In effect, he did me a favour, although I was broken-hearted at the time. Having to get married, and without even a shotgun at the wedding.

And now my husband, who would have been the father of my child, only it was all a mistake and I realised this was no time for having children, especially daughters, and with our heredity it might — she might — have been a girl. Anyhow, my husband, Donald, is playing soldiers on the esplanade of the Castle with the rest of them. Taken in by the spectacle and the noise, like everyone else. Ah, meantime, my father has disposed of his 40 winks. And I had better get the Primus stove for he insists on home cooking, which means he insists that I cook for him if anyone does.

LEAR: I dreamt I was taking part in a great show. I dreamt I was making it out of the world to an audience of thousands, more than the General Assembly gets, and then you came in on your bicycle and carried me off just before the applause!

CORDELIA: Not a moment too soon, believe me. That wee fool of yours, that little wee fellow, that spreader of gloom and despondency, he was predicting your death and his death and everybody's death. Well, all right. But then he began predicting my death and I realised I had heard enough. I was not going to let it happen. I was going to rescue you. You and I never had much to say to each other, but I wasn't going to let you slip out of the world to timultuous applause and using my lifeless body as an object of sympathy to be conferred upon you. I wasn't going to let it happen. Without a word. Without a word from me I mean. There's got to be something in it for Cordelia some day, I said. She is not just going to be something her father uses like a medal to proclaim his sores. She is getting on to her byke — I happened to have it parked in St. John's Close in the Lawnmarket. I was there seeing what they've done to the Old Traverse Theatre. Anyhow I carried you off!

LEAR: It is quite the most moving moment in all dramatic history, the speech of King Lear before he dies. Quite the most splendid achievement of any dramatist. The spectacle of a great heart, greatly opened and greatly exposed and loudly broken. Oh girl, you don't know what you did to me tonight when I realised that my understudy, and not I myself, would be making that great impassioned speech. I'd have had them without a dry eye in the house. They came along — they were certain to have come along — with the largest size in handkerchiefs. And it would have been me, and not my understudy, for how could he possibly do justice to it, good as he is at his job, how could he know what I've lived to know, how could he break his heart as I could break mine? Look at me, girl, I was made for it!

But you, because you never could stomach an unhappy ending, you never appreciated the significance, the heights attained in the tragic demise — before a full house, especially! You, you, a slip of a girl, arrive and carry your father off — me with my decent wheelchair waiting — me, you carry me off on your handlebar! It was no' even decent. It was certainly not fair!

CORDELIA: (CHEERFUL) Now father, take your hot soup. Sheep's heid broth, the way you always liked it, and this time I've scooped out all the hairs.

LEAR: Couldn't you have waited?

CORDELIA: No. The applause might have gone to your head. And that wee fool of yours just loves to play to the gallery. He would have persuaded you to do it night after night for the whole 3 weeks. Oh, I know that wee fellow! There is no feast for Feste greater than the joy he gets out of watching other folk breaking their hearts. It's a sort of revenge for his own unhappiness. I'm not blaming him, mind, but I'm not letting you get like that too. And we had the train to catch. With me having to get a nice young man I met in the Fringe Information office to run your wheelchair to the corner where I could change you over into it and give you my byke to carry so I could push your chair.

LEAR: I get more sympathy in this wheelchair, I find, than draped across a front handlebar.

CORDELIA: Your beard and the long hair; on you they're ageing.

LEAR: Which comes first, the appearance or the feeling of age? Ooh, I wish I had my wee fool here.

CORDELIA: No need, father. You do fine on your own. Or you will do fine, now you've got me. Finish your soup now.

LEAR: I'm an old man.

CORDELIA: You're 55.

LEAR: It's been a hard life.

CORDELIA: It hasn't been a life at all. You're just beginning.

LEAR: What is this place we've got to look after, daughter?

CORDELIA: It's a large old place in Wester Ross. Well away from the oil rigs. You and I are to be caretakers for the absentee landlords while they live in Switzerland to avoid the taxes.

LEAR: That sounds a sensible arrangement.

CORDELIA: You do like the country, father, do you?

LEAR: I have aye wanted to live in the country. Nature has so much to teach a man of my calibre.

CORDELIA: So I said yes, for both of us. Anyhow, we had nowhere else to go.

LEAR: What is to be our function?

CORDELIA: You are to be stationed on the hillside in a sort of sunhouse — well, it catches the sun when there is any — and people will come around and look over. You will have a quill pen and ink, and you will sign autographs.

LEAR: King Lear.

CORDELIA: Or ex-King Lear. It does not really matter.

LEAR: I shall hold audience, dear.

CORDELIA: In the season, yes.

LEAR: How far . . . north is this . . . place of ours, daughter?

CORDELIA: Quite far north, dear.

LEAR: It'll be a . . . short season?

CORDELIA: Except for the ski slopes they're starting.

LEAR: I thought the hills there would have been rather too . . .

CORDELIA: They'll flatten out the hills that are rather too . . . father.

LEAR: I had no sons, Cordelia, as you know.

CORDELIA: Yes, darling. You had just us 3 girls. It must have been a terrible disappointment.

LEAR: I could have put my sons at the head of a troop. I could have dressed them in my special tartan. I could have resuscitated a special tartan to dress them in. I could have entered them for the 3 weeks of the Tattoo. The family fortunes could have been reclaimed. There are occasions, all over the world, Cordelia girl, and not just in Ulster, for hiring out one's bands of mercenaries. There are no soldiers like Scottish soldiers. It comes from needing the money. And the Scot aye feels he needs the money. There is of course also the opportunity to get away. To travel, they call it. The Scot aye feels he needs the first opportunity he can get to get away. Look at you, for instance!

CORDELIA: I was banished, father.

LEAR: Oh I forgot that. Your sisters, dear, your sisters were not a credit to their . . . sex, if I may put it that way.

CORDELIA: What do you mean dear?

LEAR: They turned out to be worse than sons would have been. With my sons, I would have known what to expect. It would have been natural for them to grow up and want to supplant me. But Regan and Goneril, they deceived me altogether. They pretended to care what happened to me. I wouldn't have expected that from sons. But from girls, yes.

CORDELIA: (TO THE AUDIENCE) We are so different from the English. We already feel more at home now we're part of Europe. The English are far too gentle.

LEAR: They're too easily pleased, the English. I have felt more at home in Paris. Till I fell on hard times. Or rather till hard times fell on me. Paris that recognised Hume and Carlyle, recognised my logical positivism. So when I fell on hard times, I got out. I didn't know where I belonged then.

CORDELIA: Oh father, you were always so conscious of territory. What's yours is mine, you said to the foreigner, what's yours is mine and what's mine's my own. It was the family motto.

LEAR: I was aye going to bring riches back home. To astonish the neighbours. Not that you can easily astonish them! But to build my folly on Calton and set up my court in Rose Street. And now!

CORDELIA: You should not have encouraged Regan and Goneril to play at soldiers.

LEAR: They took to it so naturally. But I did enjoy drilling those girls on the esplanade. How could I know that they would take over their own platoons and turn against me, the Old Lear that they knew I was, their own father! Oh what a heredity I was offering them, Cordelia, the perpetua mobile of the power game. So what did they have to do but go on and try to win? It was most unnatural.

CORDELIA: (TO THE AUDIENCE). My husband's first thought was "If there is to be anything left to you and me Cordelia, for the time when you feel it safe to have children, we must retrieve your father's lost fortunes." "I must take my battalions", he said, "back over the seas and fight on his side. May the right side win!" But I told my husband, "No, Donald, we can win nothing nowadays by force of armour. Warfare must be psychological now." So I left him after the journey and for all I know it is he who lets off the one-o'clock gun over Princes Street. And I admit they are a beautiful body of men. My heart stirs at the music. At the pop records. And, oh, they don't do it just for the uniform. Not just for the pay.

LEAR: No doubt at all they really enjoy . . . their jobs.

CORDELIA: No doubt about it. They can learn to kill. My husband's battalion — he insists they are all of them christened. Very few of them actually join up christened, these days, that is. So my husband, he finds out whether they were christened or not. He is not narrowminded. He does not mind which persuasion — which foot, as they say, they kick off with — just so long as he gets them all christened in one church or another. We have come a long way here from narrow-mindedness. Any church will do now for the actual christenings. Just so long, my husband says, as they are ready for the Roll Call, Over There. My husband is very tidy. A very tidy man. He doesn't like any mixup. He likes at least to know that every dead man had a name. Sometimes it's as if he's balancing the books. After the battle. You follow me?

LEAR: I do not know how my wee fool is going to get on without me. I don't need him. I don't really need anybody. I am, I pride myself, selfsufficient, but that wee fool of mine, I think he is going to feel quite lost. Who is he going to turn to look at so that he knows he could be worse off? Whose misfortunes will he now be unable to avoid seeing, so that he knows he's needed? Where will he look so that he can think he's lucky? Tell me that. That little wee fellow, he'll break his heart. Wondering where to turn for someone to blame.

CORDELIA: Dearest daddy, no-one is ever at a loss for lost causes. Don't worry too much for that little wee fellow. I bet he's doing his own late night show on the fringe of the Fringe. Now let me tidy you, dear.

LEAR: I understand your enjoyment of my predicament.

CORDELIA: Oh daddy, I cannot enjoy the sight of what you've become. You've become embittered.

LEAR: Have I?

CORDELIA: You've let yourself go.

LEAR: I've had a lot to worry me. For instance, I lost your mother very early on.

CORDELIA: I lost her earlier, dear.

LEAR: I'd had her longer, so I missed her more.

CORDELIA: Why did you lose her, dear? It sounds terribly careless.

LEAR: No, no, it wasn't carelessness; she died.

CORDELIA: Oh, I'm sorry.

LEAR: Yes, she died.

CORDELIA: How did she die, dear? You never would talk about it.

LEAR: She thought I blamed her because you 3 girls were all Just Girls. She was never further from the truth. But she didn't believe that.

CORDELIA: She died of your disappointment then?

LEAR: That's how she put it. I insisted I wasn't disappointed. I insisted we had plenty of time. That I was, comparatively speaking, a young man, that I might have

5 or 6 daughters more before I could take it for granted I would never have a son. She could not be placated. So she died.

CORDELIA: She died worn out!

LEAR: Certainly not. Tended day and night, hand and foot.

CORDELIA: Oh daddy, don't be sad. Don't blame yourself.

LEAR: I am not sad! Well, yes, I am sad. But I'm not blaming myself. I am angrier, in fact, than I am sad. Your mother, my dear — you will find it difficult to believe this because I have never allowed a word of blame about your mother to pass anybody's lips, not even my own — but your mother was a terrible woman for putting other people in the wrong. She went the length . . . I can put it no more gently because I am not a man given to skirting the truth, except when it would prove rather inconvenient to face it . . . your mother died to spite me. I'm sorry, girl. It's the only mother you ever had. And she might have been nice to you, and Regan and Goneril might have benefited from having her around a lot longer. But would she wait to take the blame for what these girls became? She would not! She saw the signs, she said. And she pulled out.

CORDELIA: My mother — are you telling me that my own mother died of a broken heart?

LEAR: Nothing less!

CORDELIA: That's terrible. A terrible thing to grow up not knowing.

LEAR: Yes. And what right had she? Even at the time she died, she had no right to have her heart broken. She was younger than me. She was beautiful and I was — well, you see me. I was never very much. She used to sing and dance. She entered my establishment . . . smiling.

CORDELIA: Oh father, she didn't know what she was in for. Obviously.

LEAR: That's no excuse. No. She died so I would think it was all my fault. Well, she was much mistaken. Her death didn't teach me a thing. It took much more. She was too soft, your mother. But she never believed that. She acted as if being gentle was the way to be, I'm not going so far as to say I was glad when she died. No, no, that would be going too far. But when she did die, somebody somewhere was saying "I told you so!"

CORDELIA TRIES TO HAND HER FATHER<br>A HANDKERCHIEF

LEAR: You are quite mistaken if you think I'm in tears.

CORDELIA: I thought perhaps you were catching a cold.

LEAR: Ach well, that is just possible. I could be catching a cold. Where is the Vitamin C? A man of my age, and experience, must learn how to take care of his health. For a man of my age cannot always be sure of having a daughter around long enough to out live him. What I've noticed about old age, my dear — in myself if not in others — is the older you get the older you mean to continue getting. If I'm catching a cold, then maybe I need a tonic. Could you see to it that the guard on the train wherever you're sending me stops at Boots to get me a tonic. They know at Boots what tonic I take. I am their most regular customer. Every time I feel a stab of pain anywhere, I know I must be failing in some physical way. So I get myself a tonic. That is, I get one of my daughters, till they lose patience with me, I get one of the girls to call at Boots and get me a tonic. And Vitamin C's for extras. It never fails. In no time, the pain goes away and I wait happily for the next one. For every physical pain has a physical source. And in having a physical source, it can be physically treated. Oh, I am grateful to you, daughter, for noticing that I was catching a cold in this nasty, draughty station. Walk me up and down and tuck me well in. I am going to write a letter — no, I shall get you to write a letter to the Lord Provost. About his station. And I hope that farmhouse we're going to caretake has central heating. And that sunhouse, I hope it has sun. Oh I feel much better. I have spent the past minute or two thinking about the state of my health. It is a great tonic in itself, I find. If engaged in for some part of every day — the enumeration of the many ills which — and I quote — Flesh is Heir to — if engaged in noticing the aches and pains I have myself, I very soon find that what happens to anyone else — no matter whom — ceases to worry me. There, now, you can have your hanky back.

CORDELIA:  You've hardly used it.

LEAR:  That's quite true. And I've perked up again too at small expense. Don't stop pushing me back and forward, girl. It keeps you young, a job to do.

CORDELIA:  I had not realised how much you were enjoying it.

LEAR:  Now that is very unreasonable. When I show you the stuff of which I am made, the resilience I have to no matter what, as long as it is not happening to me, when I show you how quickly I can perk up, you accuse me of not even being an invalid!

CORDELIA:  I'm accusing you of making the most of it.

LEAR:  You are mistaken, child. I make the best of it.

CORDELIA:  Come, daddy, up out of that chair, dear. We'll walk up and down and keep each other warm.

LEAR:  I don't know if I can.

CORDELIA:  I think you can dear. Left right. Left right. Remember those soldiers drilling on the barracks square. Remember what a fine body of men they are. How handsome. How much admired.

LEAR: A man stays handsome. It's women who go to seed.

CORDELIA: That's right dear. Remember how beautiful you look when you're striding back and forth, left right. Never say die, you said. Die with the boots on, you vowed.

LEAR: Never. Never Never die at all. That's me. Take care. (LITTLE THOUGHT). Do you remember when I last . . . went, dear?

CORDELIA: The porter took you about 10 minutes ago.

LEAR: Now are you sure about that?

CORDELIA: Twenty minutes then! It was the first place you looked for when we entered the station. It was in fact the reason why we missed the train.

LEAR: Twenty minutes ago, you said.

CORDELIA: No more than twenty — yes.

LEAR: I take a note of these things.

CORDELIA: You what?

LEAR: I keep my doctor informed.

CORDELIA: But why?

LEAR: So he knows if he's prescribing the right medicine. I keep notes. There are hardly any of my bodily functions which I can quite depend on now.

CORDELIA: With that wee fool cooking your food!

LEAR: As an entertainer, a fool may have his moments, although his ideas of a joke were very questionable at times. Very questionable taste, that wee fool's jokes. But he was no cook!

CORDELIA: Well, I'll be an improvement maybe?

LEAR: At the same time, I must continue keeping my notes. 15 minues — no 20 minutes ago, no.

CORDELIA: Yes!

LEAR: And for how long would you say did I leave your side? Would you say I was gone for 2 or perhaps for 3 or 4 minutes? It all adds up. Phone the doctor! Why should he be sleeping while I lie awake?

CORDELIA: (EXASPERATED AT LAST). I know I am your daughter. I know that, no matter how badly you treated me as a child, I owe you a duty of filial affection. I know all that, father. I know that when I was a little girl you never so much as exchanged a word with me. I noticed that at the time. I mentioned it to my mother. I said, "Mummy, why does Daddy not exchange a word or two with us children? Why does he pass us looking like Napoleon?"

LEAR: He was a small man!

CORDELIA: The size of the man hardly counts!

LEAR: It makes all the difference.

CORDELIA: If you had been five feet tall, you still would not have exchanged a word with us.

LEAR: I was waiting till you were grown up.

CORDELIA: I know. My mother explained.

LEAR: In certain respects, that woman forestalled me.

CORDELIA: She said you were waiting till we were grown up enough to be worth talking to.

LEAR: An excellent woman in many respects, your mother. It's a pity she didn't last, however, to see this day. She would never have forgotten you.

CORDELIA: What I noticed was that you never exchanged a word with her either.

LEAR: Slander! I talked to the woman quite often. Whenever I could think of anything to say that she would understand.

CORDELIA: You chatted to your soldiers for hours.

LEAR: Man to man conversation. Important things to discuss.

CORDELIA: I thought I'd just make my statement,

for the record. Those notes you take. "Today my daughter Cordelia got the better of me."

LEAR: I've been forcibly ejected from the frying pan into the fire.

CORDELIA: (EAGERLY). Oh father, give me a cuddle.

LEAR: I don't know if I know how.

CORDELIA: You put your arms around me; it's easy. And I nestle nearer to you. Oh father, you're bigger than me. You were always bigger than me. I thought it was significant somehow. I thought "There will be one day when I need to cry. One day when I'll think it worthwhile crying, for my father will gather me into him closely." Only, you never did.

LEAR: Oh I must have nursed you once or twice when you were a baby.

CORDELIA: No. There was a girl I know. Her father was a foreigner. He used to bounce her, balanced on his foot. And it made a swing. Oh, what I missed, not having a father who was a . . . foreigner!

LEAR: I must have told you stories though, when you were small.

CORDELIA: No, you were always drilling your soldiers.

LEAR: Nonsense.

CORDELIA: You never told any of us stories.

LEAR: Well it would just be that I don't approve.

CORDELIA: Oh father, what do you aprove of?

LEAR: I don't approve of children going away and getting themselves an education; they're sure to use it against their father!

CORDELIA: It's better, getting answered back, father.

LEAR: I don't know.

CORDELIA: There's something you don't know? Surely that's . . . better.

LEAR: Your mother might have . . . waited.

CORDELIA: You can say anything you like against my mother now, father, for I'm not going to believe you. You only know what you're ready to know. You've a long way to go to learn . . . just like me.

LEAR: Will we farm this place we're caretaking?

CORDELIA: I'll keep hens anyway. But you? What time will you have over, from signing the autographs?

LEAR: I might farm a few sheep. One year they had sheep on at the Tatoo. With a good sheepdog.

CORDELIA: I've got to learn to milk a cow.

LEAR: I've often bought gardening books.

CORDELIA: Vegetables.

LEAR: A flower or two.

CORDELIA: I thought you didn't approve.

LEAR: A few things I didn't approve of I'm liable to change my mind about. Just don't . . . hurry me.

CORDELIA: There's an extra cottage, father, attached to the farm . . . I hoped we . . .

LEAR: We could let it. Put by a few pounds.

CORDELIA: We could not!

LEAR: Maybe invite a family of two from the city — for a holiday.

CORDELIA: Father, your wonderful!

LEAR: But I don't like children much.

CORDELIA: You could learn to like other people's children maybe.

LEAR: The responsibility wouldn't be in it.

CORDELIA: Other folks' children would keep you young, dear.

LEAR: It's your own that bring your head down with sorrow.

CORDELIA: I'm not going to have any children, father. So I've got to tend to other people's. O.K?

LEAR: And a dog. A man's got to have someone

who'd do what they're told.

CORDELIA: A habit of authority's difficult to . . . lose. Isn't it father?

LEAR: The train's in, then, is it?

CORDELIA: Will I push you up the platform.

LEAR: I'll manage, I think.

CORDELIA: You wait for me mind at Oban, where we arranged, till I get up there on my byke.

LEAR: Don't let them nudge you off the road, mind. Go on now. I don't like waving goodbye.

CORDELIA: You'll hardly have time to get there! I'm an able lady . . . your child, father.

LEAR: The conversation's we'll have, maybe. The long chats on the long evenings waiting for the Aurora Borealis.

# SOMETHING IN IT FOR OPHELIA

by

## JOAN URE

# SOMETHING IN IT FOR OPHELIA

Characters

MARTIN, HANNAH

Place:   Waverley Station, Edinburgh.

Time

The present.
(Late in the evening.)

HANNAH: You are obviously, with that high forehead, the sort of gentleman who would not speak to a young girl first, and because of that I have hardly hesitated. I said to myself, "Then Hannah you speak to him. For there is no time to be lost."

MARTIN: I am reading Wittgenstein's "Tractatus". I don't consider that wasting time. It is really rather rewarding.

HANNAH: But we have both of us, sir, 20 minutes to share before the next Glasgow train and of course from the size of your book I see you are contemplating the whole journey. The snag is, however, that I am going only as far as Falkirk.

MARTIN: Then you should be home in bed by half past eleven, o'clock.

HANNAH: Meantime, there is an opportunity which I feel ought not to be missed for a lively conversation and I feel certain you will agree with me for we both came down the hill from the same play in the same place and missed the same train by less than the same 2 minutes! Now isn't that astonishing?

MARTIN: That does not convince me that in conversation we could share any common ground. There are many people who have been to see "Hamlet" who

don't seem to have seen the same play, these days.
HANNAH: I fear it will seem churlish to you but I enjoy a good book, just as well, and a book does not answer you back, or you can close it.
HANNAH: (Laughs in the most natural but flattering way). But don't you agree that having sat opposite each other on either side of the apron stage at the Assembly Hall that is such a strange coincidence that it would really be dreadful if we could not extend the experience with a little harmless conversation?
MARTIN: Are you suggesting to me that you and I were two among those masses in that auditorium for what is perhaps the most important play by the man who was and is in my opinion the most important playwright of all time.
HANNAH: I do not agree with you. But you see how we already have found no difficulty in finding something to say.
MARTIN: You would like to discuss — is that it? — the quality of the experience you have just had?
HANNAH: Precisely!
MARTIN: May I assume that you enjoyed the play and now you want to tell me just why you enjoyed it?
HANNAH: Oh I didn't enjoy it at all. I really think it is quite shocking.
MARTIN: And am I supposed to be moved by your disappointment?
HANNAH: Oh no, not at all. We are unknown to each other. I do not expect you to feel responsible for me. But what I wondered about was would you care to discuss the play.
MARTIN: I don't know if I would. It's a play I have treasured in what I suppose someone like you might call "the heart"; that is Hamlet is a play which I now believe is part of my experience. There is this sort of

production or the other, but my "Hamlet" is safe. (He is tapping his chest with a more theatrical gesture than he would have allowed himself, except this young girl is making him feel personally "attacked").

HANNAH: (Very humbly and sweet). But although I have the Woman's Friend, I do not enjoy a magazine as much as I used to. I think I have somewhat outgrown magazine-type literature and anyhow there are only the short stories left to read and I do not approve of fiction. So I thought you might help me with my puzzlement about the play. I could not understand all the applause. I thought it was really shocking. I know it was just a play, but to be honest, I am very much distressed after it, and if I don't get it off my chest a bit, if you will excuse the frivolity of the expression, I will not be able to sleep.

MARTIN: And you must get your sleep?

HANNAH: For the sake of my complexion.

MARTIN: Ah, yes. That is a reason.

HANNAH: (Brightening, for she is winning him round, she believes). And, if we waited until the train actually came in we would not have so long for discussion, whereas if we began now, it would not then be so likely, if our conversation developed momentum — as conversations so often do and that is what is so delightful, that in spite of all, we could not dispose of it, sew it up and tuck it away so that by the time I have to get off and leave you to your loneliness for the rest of the journey, it could really be rather nice, and we might never see each other again!

MARTIN: That has the makings of the sort of invitation that has merits I recognise.

HANNAH: (Very happy) There! We are beginning quite beautifully!

MARTIN: (Takes off his reading glasses and sees the

pretty, eager young girl). Would it really increase your enjoyment of this evening to talk?

HANNAH: It would most certainly add to the profit that I would be taking home with me to Falkirk.

MARTIN: A work of art is sufficient in itself.

HANNAH: I don't know about that, except if that's true, why are you not just sitting?

MARTIN: (Signalling to the book). A form of self-defence.

HANNAH: Oh, I see, you're shy!

MARTIN: No.

HANNAH: Now don't malign yourself. You're shy. And if I had not spoken to you, you might have had no-one to speak to! Oh I really feel I have been useful. I begin to feel much better already.

MARTIN: Are you perhaps sitting your A levels? If that is so, would it not be more profitable to you and less exhausting for me if you were to talk about the play you have just seen one version of with your English teacher? Then you could divide it up into examinable categories and what it had to say would not come into it at all.

HANNAH: I am 20 years of age. I will even be 21 on Saturday next. I have been working in the Royal Bank of Scotland with a grill of my own over the past 4 months, in Elmwood Street. It is therefore quite some time since I sat and obtained, mind you, A levels in 6 subjects.

MARTIN: In 6 . . .

HANNAH: Yes.

MARTIN: You did not fail in anything?

HANNAH: I succeed in everything that will rebound to my credit. I winkle away till I get at it. It is a family failing. (She waits for him to laugh. He does smile, and nods acknowledgement of her wit). That is not my own turn of phrase. I must be honest.

MARTIN: Oh a pity.

HANNAH: But I inherited it. It is one of the several things my mother's mother used to say to astonish us children at the breakfast table while we were supposed to save our breath to cool our porridge.

MARTIN: You had a mother's mother who rose determinedly with the lark.

HANNAH: Oh when she liked she could be entertaining, too, but there were other days when she was not speaking to any of us. She said often that she was not very fond of children; perhaps that's why my mother's so quiet. Children, my grandma said, were so liable to interrupt. And their conversational chitchat was very limited.

MARTIN: I agree with your grandmother.

HANNAH: It was not that we lacked the vocabulary, she said. It was what we tortured the vocabulary into as soon as we got hold of it. I could see at once that you are rather a moody person, rather prone to boredom, and that therefore if our conversation was to make headway, I should open with my grandmother as soon as I could.

MARTIN: I will get no sleep in the train, I foresee.

HANNAH: After Falkirk, you can sleep as much as you like.

MARTIN: Thank you for that dispensation.

HANNAH: I can see that you are a very sensitive and perceptive person trying hard to pretend that you're not.

MARTIN: I confess!

HANNAH: I suppose you are as Scots as I am?

MARTIN: I don't mind, if you don't. To rephrase that, I don't mind anyway! I myself prefer foreigners; there's always the myth that they had an easier time and that makes one feel superior.

HANNAH:  No one would ever guess where either of us came from by the way we talk. Don't you find that such a comfort?

MARTIN:  I don't mind who knows that I came from Glasgow.

HANNAH:  It's the going back at night that's uncomfortable. Some very nice Americans who come into the bank — they keep their hair very short — very good clients of the manager's, they take out enormous loans and he just loves that. You get upgraded you see, dependent on the number of large loans people take out.

MARTIN:  That doesn't seem to influence them in Glasgow.

HANNAH:  O go on, you're not listening at all. But they are very welcome clients of ours, as I was trying to impress upon you, and it was they who drew my attention to the fact that I had no accent. And I said to them as I say to you, only don't you take offence too, that we do not all have to talk with an accent. Of course I expect you can guess, they thought I was referring obliquely to their own quaint sort of twang, but I would not be so rude or presumptuous.

MARTIN:  You would not intend to be, I'm certain.

HANNAH:  I do get on very well with people.

MARTIN:  Good for you.

HANNAH:  That is why I do not understand Ophelia. For she was younger than me, supposed to be. How then could she get like that, so soon? No, I don't mean so soon. I mean how can anyone get like that. It's not as if she had lost all her chances; there were plenty young men about that court. I really have little sympathy. I call that letting yourself go. It is very extravagant behaviour. I can't help wondering how she was brought up. And yet Polonius, if you remember, her father, he was very much like anybody else's father, except of course he dressed a bit different. But Ophelia, she embarrassed me. I mean I don't mind what the men do, or the older women. But what the young girls do sort of reflects upon oneself. I really had little sympathy. If she were my sister, for instance, and thank God she is not, but if she were I wouldn't know where to look.

MARTIN:   Her heart was presumed to be broken.

HANNAH:  What   nonsense!  They   weren't   even engaged!

MARTIN:   Perhaps you have just been fortunate.

HANNAH:  I have had no experience, of that sort, whatever, and at that rate, I am not at all likely. But even so, and apart from me altogether, she was really rather an unbalanced sort of a person. Surely. Even for a person in a play, which I admit is largely fiction and not to be taken too seriously. But up on that rostrum, well it's difficult to remember a thing like that. I was — I admit it — I was humiliated!

MARTIN:   Humiliated!

HANNAH:  Yes, I blushed. I don't often blush, but I blushed.

MARTIN:   That girl's father had been murdered.

HANNAH:  Look at the number of road deaths!

MARTIN:   And murdered by her own lover. Not by a Triumph TN2.

HANNAH:  Well of course if he was her lover! Honestly as if that made it better!

MARTIN:   What do you mean by that?

HANNAH:  If she let herself be led astray by an older man — well. Pononius had told her, as you know, that because Hamlet spoke her fair once or twice, she would have been a fool ... if ... But of course if she was a fool, well then.

MARTIN:   Are you quite heartless?

HANNAH: I really think people make their own beds these days.

MARTIN: What do you mean by "these days." We are in this play referring to "those days".

HANNAH: You put it on a stage in these days, and you cannot honestly say that it stays referring to those days? People make their own beds anyway. It really does not make much difference. If I were to meet an Ophelia right now after I got off the train, once it comes, if I were to, I honestly would not know where to look.

MARTIN: It could never happen to you?

HANNAH: I find that an abominable suggestion. I doubt very much that I've given you the least excuse. Hamlet, like yourself, was a very much older man.

MARTIN: You see — I shall not refer to your suggestion about myself — but I shall keep within the frame of reference of the play which we set ourselves the task of discussing, you see Hamlet as "an older man".

HANNAH: 32 or perhaps 33 — I mean I've read the play; it's just though when you see it that it begins to hurt you . . . I mean on the page you can ignore these things, except for examination purposes and we all know that's just so that one gets a good job, but I have also read the play, and I distinctly remember . . . 32 or 33 and Ophelia 17 if I remember. Younger than me, in fact. Double her age, Hamlet was. I never could understand it. We all know that an older man can be attracted by a young girl, or at least by a younger woman, but it cannot happen the other way round. I mean that's why I spoke to you. I knew you could never imagine anything improper because nothing improper could have been possible, instigated by myself that is. Whereas, as I mentioned at the time, you could hardly — in all propriety — speak to me in case I suspected your intentions, so that was why I had to speak to you. Hamlet being an older man also, I wondered if you could perhaps explain. Because I am frankly bewildered.

MARTIN: Do you mind if we do not say anything more about Hamlet for the moment, till I . . . I agree that Hamlet is a man who feels his age. I agree as far as that.

HANNAH: Such bad taste. Jumping in and out of the grave, too. Our minister would have a fit. I can just imagine what he would say. No, I cannot imagine what he would say! I cannot even contemplate it without blushing. I doubt if I ever have blushed so much about anything. I cannot really approve of that sort of thing happening in our own General Assembly Halls. And do you know this, my young sister is going with their whole Sunday School class? I really think I must mention it to the minister. And yet how is one to approach a subject of that sort. I could say that everyone was showing off.

MARTIN: Everyone was. . . .

HANNAH: Jumping about and carrying on. Oh please I don't really want to talk about it! I think perhaps I am quite right; I have always been embarrassed by the idea of fiction. My father has always warned us against too much fiction. I believe plays must be classed as fiction. Keep the feet on the ground, my father says, there are already too many facts.

MARTIN: There are, yes.

HANNAH: So why worry our heads with fictions?

MARTIN: Just because there are too many unpalatable facts.

HANNAH: And do you mean to tell me that the play we just saw made unpalatable facts less unpalatable?

MARTIN: In a way, I do mean that, yes.

HANNAH: Do you know that in the summer there the sociologists were rather alarmed — it said in The Scotsman, "rather alarmed", because we've got about as high a suicide rate, that's what they said, as high as Sweden only most of ours are females. Isn't that horribly unwholesome? Not old females, either. Just females. Do you know what that suggests, that suggests me! I really object to that sort of thing. I am absolutely certain that was a fiction which the sociologists resorted to. Because if it was not a fiction that someone was resorting to then it is hardly fair to publish it and frighten people, people who are females themselves. You know I remembered that bit from the Scotsman when I saw that Ophelia. And do you know that when the lights went up and I looked round it was as if all the men were Hamlet. They were clapping and clapping too. I got very frightened then. I had to remind myself of a few things. My own father's name, Maxwell Macnair, my brother's name, Rutherfor Macnair. I kept saying all the names of boys and men I knew, so that I wouldn't be turning my head and seeing everybody clapping and clapping because they were seeing themselves as Hamlet.

MARTIN: My name is Martin Armstrong. Don't say anything more for a minute. I've been seeing myself as Hamlet for years. Give me a few moments to recover. I had not realised it was a crime.

HANNAH: I'm glad you see it now though.

MARTIN: You think that the next young female who tries to kill herself anywhere may be doing it because of something about me?

HANNAH: Oh that sounds terrible.

MARTIN: Am I responsible for a female somewhere?

HANNAH: Here. Yes here. You are.

MARTIN: Why do you say that?

HANNAH: I don't know why. I don't really believe it.

I believe one makes one's own bed.

MARTIN: What you almost allowed yourself to say, however, was that I might make your bed for you.

HANNAH: Oh no, because you are an older man.

MARTIN: Oh yes, I am an older man.

HANNAH: Well no, but you are rather more mature.

MARTIN: Being an older man is not being Hamlet. being an older man is being Hamlet's father.

HANNAH: Oh, I'm sorry.

MARTIN: Yes.

HANNAH: If you saw all the young girls clapping and clapping, could you believe they were clapping and clapping because you were dead?

MARTIN: Is that how it felt?

HANNAH: Yes. And I was frightened.

MARTIN: You never felt that sort of thing before?

HANNAH: I am 20 years old.

MARTIN: Of course, you are only 20 years old.

HANNAH: Do you really mind my having talked to you. I did it, I took the risk because I was frightened.

MARTIN: Frightened of what.

HANNAH: Frightened in case no man would take time and trouble to talk to me.

MARTIN: And it mattered to you?

HANNAH: Yes, it mattered to me an awful lot. You see I don't do embroidery. And I haven't got a nunnery to be banished to. Not unless I turn. And I really could not genuinely turn. You understand. There are so many people you can hurt by turning. I mean no offence to you if you are a Catholic but if you are you may know what I mean the other way around. You would not, for instance turn Church of Scotland. For your mother would look down and reproach you. Well that's how I'd feel about going into a nunnery. My mother well she doesn't have to look down because she

is still alive, and for your sake I very much hope that
your mother even if she is rather an old lady, I very
much hope that she is still alive. But people can just
turn because other people have banished them into
nunneries. So one gets distraught. Wondering what one
will do if the like of something like that occurs. I think
I had to get angry with Ophelia for fear I'd sympathise
too much. It would be an unmanageable world if one
were to sympathise too much.

MARTIN: Why do you think I sit in stations and
instead of seeking out people as you do, I read and read
in books?

HANNAH: I was wondering why you did that. People
are so much more interesting.

MARTIN: I do it because I cannot manage in a world
peopled by too many of myself. I have never had any
difficulty identifying with people. My difficulty has
been in keeping people out. All right then, I am causing
some female somewhere to attempt to commit suicide
and why, you tell me it is because I won't discuss plays
with her. You tell me that if I don't make a bed for
some female, that female will not be able to make a
bed for herself. I have known that was the case. We are
all, I have told myself, guilty. It has been a species of
consolation. I have marched up and down platforms in
stations from Glasgow Queen Street to Edinburgh
Waverley and at times I have convinced myself that if a
female somewhere is trying to commit suicide it
honestly has nothing to do with me because I never talk
to females.

HANNAH: It's mostly young females I am concerned
with. Older females nearly all seem to be married and
once they are married it soon seems to them all right
that men hardly ever talk to them but the young females
go off somewhere and try to commit suicide.

MARTIN: I will not be made responsible. I do not care if you start naming names. I know, over the years, I have been inclined to see myself as Hamlet, with the world to put right in a fortnight when all the time one has is a week. And choices have had to be made — that has seemed inevitable. But I really, quite honestly, believed that Ophelia was a convenient fiction, a rather fine part for a girl with not too many lines to learn and a chance for a fine bit of acting. But you find it makes you blush. And you feel that there is something I ought to do about it, because you belong to the Church of Scotland. You make life very difficult for me. It took me years to leave my mother's flat — my mother lives in Dennistoun, in a red sandstone tenement building, in a very good state of repair. I worked hard and now I teach. I teach physics as it happens. It has not solved very much, because I could never convince my mother that the reason I wished to live in a flat of my own meant no slur upon her cooking. I never visit my mother now — my father has been dead for years — I never visit my mother for, no matter how hard she tries, she cannot help the tears and from the moment I enter the door to the moment I leave as soon as I decently can, phrases come to her lips like a sort of froth to illustrate no other thing than that she is lonely without me. There is nothing I can say about the good works she should do for other people, for there are people everywhere suffering, there is only one person she wants to do things for and that one person is me (He is weeping).

That her love is a sort of bloodsucking, that she throws her misery in my face, oh that never occurs to her. She sucks my vitality away and calls what she does to me love. She is convinced, my mother is, that she loves me. She was convinced that she loved my father. But all she meant by that was that we should never know happiness unless she gave it to us for dinner. Do you think if I rushed over there now and my face was all aglow. Not that it often is: I am more inclined to brood; but if I rushed in all aglow, she would either think I'd been drinking or else she'd take offence. Now love would mean she'd be glad. If my eyes lit up, that she'd smile. But that is not what love means to mothers, not to mothers like mine.

What love means to mothers like mine is that you sit quite still in your bed while she turns down the clean sheets and sends for the doctor and serves you meals on a tray. Love to mothers like mine means you never do anything brave or anything generous or anything great because then she wouldn't know what to expect. If ever you go home to your mother — if you have a mother like mine — and you happen to mention something which you have not mentioned to her before, she looks at you as if what you mean to do is keep something from her. Oh it may be that you have filled a suitcase with a recital of every other thing but it will be the one event which you forget to recount which will be the only event she is interested in.

Oh Hannah Macnair, if I really did have to believe that there is Ophelia somewhere who cannot make her bed for herself, I would throw myself in front of the train that's due in a few minutes to take me to Glasgow and you as far as Falkirk. There really must not be these helpless faces looking at one with their fine eyes and begging one never to leave them.

Oh Hannah Macnair, I was once so far gone because of just such a look, although I knew I would not love the same face by the following Tuesday, that I got myself engaged and I had to change my job — I had to move to the other side of the city — I had to disappear without a trace because I knew of the impossible expectations that

could be aroused in just such fine eyes and because I
knew that while she thought I was breaking her heart
the sight of her grief would really be breaking mine.

I am a coward in front of fine eyes, oh Hannah Macnair
and then what happens, you a young woman of 20
summers, summers and winters now too, you assure me,
insist on telling me that there is nothing in it here for
Ophelia and what am I going to do? You set impossible
talks you young girls with unfailing pertinacity. You are
wicked and you are cruel. And then you turn your
innocent eyes upon me and I know how helpless you are
and I have not the heart to tell you that you are no
more helpless than I am myself. You look at me as if I
ride a white and gold horse, and lo I am riding a white
and gold horse!

All I wanted to do was read my book. But now you
have put in my protection every young female whose
attempted suicide is caused by my reading books instead
of speaking to her, and you have no idea what you are
doing. Or that I'd never do such a thing to you.

HANNAH: If there is anything I cannot see unmoved it
is a man in tears. I don't think I have ever seen such a
thing in fact. I was always under the impression that
such a thing never occurred. I will gladly lend you my
handkerchief and in fact you may take it home; it has
my initials on it and I really think you ought to keep
my initials to remind you of this experience. It is by no
means certain when you will cry in public again. I find
myself strangely moved. I never expected to see a grown
man cry. I have spent the evening watching a grown man
jump in and out of a grave, and now I am granted the
very moving spectacle of you Martin Armstrong crying.
I really owe you a great deal.

MARTIN: So that is what I've become. I admit to you
that I do not remember the last time I was in tears. I

will have to travel tearstained in a train; it is worse than having no ticket, but to you it is a memorable experience.

HANNAH: If you would prefer me to forget it, then of course I will do so.

MARTIN: Till you reduced me to the spectacle I have become, it was you yourself who was in a terrible state.

HANNAH: However I now feel fine. It is the fact that you are so much worse off than I am myself.

MARTIN: And that, instead of paralysing you, as you were making certain it paralysed me when I began to feel for you, that feeling makes you better.

HANNAH: I suddenly am of use. Even that I had a handkerchief, it all seems prearranged.

MARTIN: (In comic anguish) There really is nothing that could kill you, Oh Hannah Macnair. No wonder that just a few of you find you have to take your own lives. The real miracle is that more girls like you do not provoke more men like me to murder.

HANNAH: This is becoming rather extravagant behaviour. I know you will be ashamed. I suggest that we each walk up and down the platform and that we meet again in a minute or two to exchange notes. I will, if you think it will help, also lend you a pencil and I always carry small notebooks. I sell them for charity but in this case you may have one on me. I'll see you back here in a minute.

MARTIN: Perhaps you could make it a minute and a half. I might get myself a sandwich. I get hungry when I'm upset.

HANNAH: No need. I've got some biscuits. With butter.

MARTIN: Now that really is very thoughtful. Very thoughtful indeed.

HANNAH: (as they meet again) I do not think the

porter or that rather suspicious inspector who had been watching us for some time I do not think they noticed anything odd. Perhaps if I had been the one who was crying, they would have felt it worth investigating. With you, they were probably rather embarrassed.

MARTIN: I cannot really blame them.

HANNAH: I think it rather heardhearted nevertheless.

MARTIN: You'd have come swarming round like a crow at a funeral. Looking for hot baked meats cold.

HANNAH: I can see you're more than a little distraught. Shall we sit down again?

MARTIN: If you don't mind I'll stride back and forth for a little. My strides at least look manly. I find that a great consolation.

HANNAH: And while you walk up and down and keep yourself warm, I'll read you what I've made of our little situation.

MARTIN: You cluster like a newspaper reporter. It's quite obvious what the situation is. You began our "chat" brokenhearted. And it has now reached the point where I suffer instead.

HANNAH: If you doubt my sympathy, you really know little about me.

MARTIN: You have passed on your distress, and that's that. I am successfully lumbered with it. No wonder I prefer to read a book. While I sat there more or less coping with the world, more or less saying to myself "All right it's hell but we love one another or die" you could give me no peace till I felt lumbered, lumbered with whether or not there would ever be anything in it for you, carrying your paltry burden, feeling it grow to unmanageable proportions. Now what I feel is "It's hell loving one another for we love one another and die". And as I cracked up, you healed. It was exactly as if I were at home. Balancing along a wall,

I felt as if I owned not just the wall but the world. I could maybe not take on all the world's problems, I felt, but that was only through lack of time. Balancing there, I know I could do quite a lot. Then my mother's face at the window calling to me "Fall down off that wall and then I'll have such a lot to do with the bandages. Fall down off that wall, boy, at once!" She did the same to my father.

HANNAH:   I feel sure you malign your mother. Mothers don't call out things like that.

MARTIN:   They don't have to say a word. There's a gleam in their eyes as they rush alongside the ambulance. They were made for just this, they are signalling. Look at us now, we are needed. Look at us now, we can't be replaced.

HANNAH:   I do not like to contradict you. I have noticed you are in years at least what they call a mature man. But I've never used expressions like that about my mother. I am not suggesting that you should feel ashamed. I am just asking you to note the comparison. I am 20 years old and unmoved. You are at least 32 and I had to lend you my handkerchief. The scene has become extravagant. I really will not know where to look.

MARTIN:   I knew when you began to speak. I knew there was this danger. That I would recognise your pain and collapse under it.

HANNAH:   You really must pull yourself together.

MARTIN:   She will tell me, I told myself, how badly life is treating her. She will not rest till she has driven me to the point where she only has to look at me to see that for me things are even worse. And then — God help us all — she will feel better. For Hamlet, she felt nothing. He was showing off. Polonius was killed by accident, and yet he was the girl's own father. Gertrude she never even mentioned.

HANNAH: Older women get on rather well, it seems to me.

MARTIN: But Ophelia — she will see to it that no-one sends Hannah Macnair to a nunnery, because she is Church of Scotland.

HANNAH: It hurts one's relations if you turn.

MARTIN: So for Ophelia, provision must be made. Ophelia must not "let herself go" like them!

HANNAH: I find the matter a little extravagant. All I wanted was some minutes discussion so that when the bank party go to the play, I myself shall have something to contribute to the discussion with my argument tried out on someone. I only wanted something to contribute.

MARTIN: Well now you can contribute me.

HANNAH: I shall not breathe a word about you. I would never give a mature man away. Crying in the station in the company of a young girl is really not something I could talk about although I admit it's your own business.

MARTIN: It's your fault.

HANNAH: I cannot allow you to say that. You know that there must have been something else, or else nothing I could say would have contributed.

MARTIN: So this was all done in the interests of morning coffee discussion.

HANNAH: We like a good argument — we do it every year at Festival time. Go to things and then compare notes. It is impossible to be bored. Shall I tell you something? I am really rather glad you disgraced yourself. I am really going to be rather glad. Because I notice that when I meet a mature man and he does not disgrace himself, I find that I dream about him. Now there is no risk that I'll dream about you.

MARTIN: I could be only a lesson to you. I wouldn't

fit into a dream.

HANNAH: Exactly. I shall remind myself that this is what comes of reading books. I shall be firmer in my conviction that to avoid fiction is something of a duty. For there you were reading some romantic novel, the Tractatus by Wittgen Stein. And next time any sociologists try to tell me that more young females even here try to end their lives than men do, I shall not be disturbed at all because I shall know they have resorted to fiction.

MARTIN: One does it in self-defence.

HANNAH: Precisely. It is a sign of weakness of character.

MARTIN: No doubt.

HANNAH: I owe you a lot Mr. Armstrong. I owe you a great deal. I shall not dream I am being supported by you, clinging as I might have done to your greater strength. I shall nail my young hopes to the mast.

MARTIN: The mast.

HANNAH: I· shall nail my hopes to something that won't burst into tears at the least strain. Do not reproach yourself, Mr. Armstrong. I shall sleep tonight rather well.

And in the morning, I'll tell the minister. I'll tell him what is going on. That Ophelia is not a typical specimen. That my sister and I would never go around like them. But that I think a petition should be drawn up for next year so that something more wholesome be urged to take place in the Assembly Hall. My father says that once they put on "The Three Estates". And that, as he says, is a very fine wholesome entertainment. You know where you are about right and wrong and it would be a more fitting offering. Because what you may not know, with you being a Catholic, or whatever it is you are for I can see you are not Church of Scotland for, though I mean no reproach, the men in the church of Scotland do not cry in public nor in private except in the case of an immediate bereavement and even then not always. They would not behave in any extravagant way, jumping in and out of graves showing off in very bad taste too.

MARTIN:   It may have been so as not to cry.

HANNAH: I really do not know what to make of you. At one moment you are just sitting as if nothing can stir you. Then the next I have to lend you my hankie. I suppose that's what comes of being moody but although we have an uncle in our family who is moody he never cries.

MARTIN:   Oh please. Miss Macnair.

HANNAH: Call me by my christian name please. Call me by my christian name.

MARTIN:   Church of Scotland christian name, Hannah Macnair. Hannah.

HANNAH: It is very difficult to know what to do in any given circumstances. Maybe I can admit that to you.

MARTIN:   Admit a weakness, oh Miss Macnair.

HANNAH: It is the only time I am driven . . . do you know I never did like people to cry. I can put on a good show. I can lend my handkerchief. But I really do not know what to do. Except with very little babies. You just walk up and down with them. But as soon as people begin to speak. Do you know what I do. You will hardly believe it. I find myself resorting to fictions! I find myself saying anything. If snapping them out of it is impossible, I find myself resorting to fictions. When my wee sister or my brother Rutherfor would cry — now I would not like you to give me away — I would find myself resorting to fictions. I'd tell them the moon was on its way. Anything. It is heartbreaking. You see?

MARTIN:   Yes, I see.

HANNAH: If I cannot pretend they are making it up and not crying really but only looking for sympathy then. . . . I find I resort to fictions.

MARTIN: And if they are only looking for sympathy, don't you ever believe that's what they're needing?

HANNAH: I cannot afford to. Oh Mr. Armstrong. What is one to do. Oh Mr. Armstrong, it is quite some time now since I stopped being able to read the papers; the fictions in there are not very entertaining.

MARTIN: Often not entertaining at all.

HANNAH: Also, Mr. Armstrong, you are rather charming. I expect you did not know that. I expect you thought that nobody could find anything charming about you. But I can.

MARTIN: You intend to see yourself as generous, I can see that.

HANNAH: Also you say rather witty things, occasionally. That is a gift, Mr. Armstrong. I myself have very little sense of humour. That, I know, you will find difficult to believe, but every scrap of humour I have got I have had to scrape up from a deep down place or else I am tempted more and more to resort to fictions.

I mean one day people will find out! And I won't know where to look. I didn't even resort to fictions when I had by mistake been doing something wrong; I used to tell the truth then and I was generally let off with a caution. That is my father's turn of phrase. "Let the girl off with a caution; she will soon learn."

MARTIN: You have a Solomon for a father, Miss Macnair.

HANNAH: Oh call me Hannah for that's my christian name.

MARTIN: I didn't know that anyone had a christian name any more.

HANNAH: You really are quite entertaining, Mr. Armstrong.

Joan Ure

'Something In It For Cordelia'

MARTIN: Thank you Miss Macnair. I had not looked at the matter that way.

HANNAH: I can turn you into a fiction, Mr. Armstrong, with a single turn of the screw. I am speaking metaphorically.

MARTIN: You have a great talent there, Miss Macnair.

HANNAH: Yes, I can tell myself that Mr. Martin Armstrong is really a fiction I met in Waverley station waiting for the 11 p.m.

MARTIN: Is it really so easy?

HANNAH: Yes, I'll write you down in my notebook and by the time I've reached about page 3, I'll have tidied you neatly away.

MARTIN: Miss Macnair, you are a monster.

HANNAH: It is a matter of self-defence. You should not have started crying. Either I turn you into a fiction or else I might be to blame.

MARTIN: Have you ever seen the Tatoo, Hannah?

HANNAH: I am so glad you have decided to call me Hannah. It keeps me sort of young. And I have seen the Tatoo 13 times. I went at first with the family, all wrapped up in tartan rugs. There are sheep on the esplanado this year. I think that would have been a better outing for the bank party.

MARTIN: But you went by yourself, tonight.

HANNAH: I went because the bank party is going later.

MARTIN: And you don't like to be left out of the discussion.

HANNAH: People think you never go anywhere.

MARTIN: You are very much influenced by what other people think.

HANNAH: That's why I got worried about Ophelia. It seemed to me so was she.

MARTIN: I could have been somewhere getting drunk. But no, I'm here, listening to you.

HANNAH: You know as well as I do that the licensing hours of this country forbid drinking in taverns after 10. I am not naive. I do know what goes on in taverns and it all stops at 10 o'clock.

MARTIN: A tavern is what you see in a coloured postcard.

HANNAH: You cannot deflect me from talk of right and wrong by discussion of the licensing hours or criticism of my vocabulary, you are just like Ophelia — you are very easily . . . offended.

MARTIN: Offended, Left right. Left right. Offended. To you everybody is manipulable. Like your moody uncle. Or is offended . . . like Ophelia! Offended — Ophelia! I believe you do not think at all. I believe that conversation with you is a sort of spontaneous combustion, a way to keep out the cold. Haven't you heard of anybody getting hurt? Grieved. Life engraves its lessons on some people. That's what adds those lines to the face and scoops the flesh away eventually.

People who take offence have a fine way out. Left right, left right. They can get angry! They can as you would no doubt express it, hit out, hit back, knock flat.

With you there's a right and wrong side. Well there is, but it refers to taking one course or another; it does not distinguish between the amount of hurt caused to people, some of whom can even be on the wrong side!

People get hurt but they understand it is inevitable or else they are hardly alive. Nobody means to hurt you. One man's need is some girl's deprivation. And vice versa. Oh people like . . . us suffer. Like Hamlet.

HANNAH: It was Ophelia who . . . drowned . . . who . . . I think she should have remembered her father.

MARTIN: He was dead. He had been murdered.

HANNAH: Hamlet didn't mean it.

MARTIN: He behaved abominably to her, her sexual energy was a provocation.

HANNAH: She should not have been taken in. She was just a simple, perhaps rather stupid girl, I suppose, poor thing.

MARTIN: They have drained our energy away, Hannah. There are too many causes. How can one choose?

HANNAH: At least I could look around afterwards, I told myself, and there were very interesting faces and some beautiful saris and costumes. People at this time come to the Athens of the North from all over.

MARTIN: Edinburgh. They come to Edinburgh.

HANNAH: My father says it is no exaggeration to call Edinburgh, a naturally very beautiful city, the Athens of the North. Of course we have a very violent history. A very violent past. Did you ever marry, Mr. Armstrong?

MARTIN: I never married, Miss Macnair.

HANNAH: I think that is really a waste. Some nice middleaged woman. My father says every man should marry, then we'd all be in the same boat.

MARTIN: We are all in the same boat, Miss Macnair.

HANNAH: Don't go to sleep Mr. Armstrong. I hear our train coming in. You can have a nice rest on the train. Come, Mr. Armstrong, it's no time to lie down and not there. There are draughts, in railway stations. Oh Mr. Armstrong, speak to me, please. I know my invariable good nature is very trying to moody people, but you really should not go into the huff. Not with the train coming. I cannot afford to miss it, because of my complexion.

# SEVEN CHARACTERS OUT OF THE DREAM

by

## JOAN URE

# SEVEN CHARACTERS OUT OF THE DREAM

Scene: A Fancy Dress party where actors have been invited to arrive as the characters they have played in a Midsummer Night's Dream by William Shakespeare.

Characters

HELENA, PUCK, TITANIA, OBERON, CHANGELING BOY, MAN AS ASS, GIRL AS LION

As the lights go up the cast in costume wend their part-
joyful, part-sinister way across the acting area. HELENA
detaches herself. The others move on. HELENA is carrying a telephone with a long festooned flex, as if she's
carried the phone out from indoors, which in fact she
has. She beckons to the CHANGELING BOY to stand
somewhere to hold the phone flex and see that the
dancing actors do not trip over it, smiling her thanks.

HELENA (to phone) But come! Drop everything.
Unless it's alive. Bottom, you're beautiful. A vast
improvement!
   (BOTTOM replies Hee Haw. Otherwise ignores her)
(to phone) All you need is what you wore in last
summer's production of the Dream.
The Dream by William Shakespeare. I wasn't suggesting
you didn't know. I thought it very likely that you
couldn't hear me.
I can't hear you!
(to actors) Oh go away, all of you. I came out here to
telephone. Don't you recognise it's a way of escape for
someone who isn't exactly enjoying her own party?
Rather than inflict oneself on one's friends, one lifts the
phone.

(to phone) It was Puck's scatter-brained idea. No we agreed to stick to our fictional names. So I'm not to say. Not about anyone. We are practically unrecognisable anyway — we hope.

(to someone passing) Darling, you look divine. Younger, if anything.

(to phone) Puck? Oh he is Puck because he sees it as the role most suited to his rather ambiguous personality. In fact he's here. Was. Is somewhere.

   (Puck is standing behind her. Everyone else is gone) Everybody is! of course it's a small house. But couldn't you join us?

Helena of course.

I know, sweetie, you have played in several productions because you went on professionally but I did not.

I gave it up. Work for my living now.

(PUCK mimes that she is a typist, within her sight now) HELENA (contd.) Helena was my last role. Couldn't stick it out. Being more out of work than in can't be good for the character. It is an old-fashioned concept, character, but my grandmother was a Scot and I am stuck with having a character and knowing it. No, I was actually saying that at Puck.

(She signals "Do you want to speak?" he signals "No"). The point is to come, sweetie, as what you were in the Dream last summer when we did it for the University. Yes, that's exactly what I'm saying. In fancy dress. We all are.

PUCK (not particularly quietly) You have to spell it out)

HELENA (to phone) It had to be something out of Shakespeare. Well chiefly because everyone who has played in anything at all has played in Shakespeare. Well why not The Dream, for heaven's sake.

PUCK (quite loudly) It seemed suitable for a party

which, if the weather had held, might have been out here in the garden.

HELENA (to phone)   Yes, that's why?

PUCK (lifting the phone from Helena)   Also it's Shakespeare so that everybody else knows who everybody is supposed to be. That is everybody has a past and it's recognisable as a past and not a guilt complex.

(gives HELENA the phone back)

HELENA (to phone)   Puck.

PUCK   Only it's just a little bit cold.

HELENA (to phone)   Did you hear?

Most of us are remaining in the house. To hear myself talk. Well don't you like the idea of the grotesques? Of the fairies then?

(PUCK does a hand on hip walk. HELENA giggles)

HELENA (to phone)   Those   marvellous   legendary creatures from the Fairy Kingdom, which are both so symbolic and so out of this world. Such a relief! We're all fed up with the world as it is. Too much television documentary, I think. No, I'm already dressed up.

PUCK (loudly)   For instance, we admit that we are fiction.

HELENA   The party's been sort of going for a little time. I'm here all the time. It's mine ... well Mummy's house, and she's away.

(PUCK skips around to show how the mice do play)

As Helena. Why not Helena? It's my part. It's me. And it was just about the last thing I ... You played Hippolyta. It must have been another production where you played Hermia. Yes, she is rather a bore of a character nowadays. Plays everything so much for real.

PUCK (mimicking Hermia)   Nay, good Lysander, for my sake, my dear lie further off yet, do not lie so near.

HELENA (mimicking Lysander)   O, take the sense sweet of my innocence.

PUCK (as Hermia again) But gentle friend for love and courtesy lie further off, in human modesty.

HELENA (listening to phone but with mouthpiece covered till she can control her laughter at PUCK) (to phone) I do not think you should come as Titania. Titania is here already as herself.

(PUCK imitates the Grande Actress)

Well, if you need to wash your hair, sweetie. No Theseus. We only have a constitutional monarchy etcetera Puck says. Just a sort of pageant really, Puck says. A habit pattern really like sucking the thumb.

(PUCK takes the phone out of her hand, replaces it, and banishes CHANGELING BOY with whole phone arrangement)

HELENA (still talking, but no longer holding the phone) It's sort of salutary to have someone to look up to.

PUCK And relieves of responsibility. (Change of tone) Are you, fair Helena, out here alone murmuring sweet nothings on the telephone?

HELENA One does what other folk are want to do, If your Demetrius has run out on you.

One hopes the telephone is magic. It hardly ever is.

PUCK What you need for your Demetrius.

HELENA Would that he were!

PUCK A single drop of juice upon his eyelid and there's an aphrodisiac for a quid.

HELENA (dropping the too difficult attempt to rhyme) Demetrius needs no aphrodisiac.

PUCK What's your complaint then?

HELENA: Maybe I need an aphrodisiac. I just love him. I think what's wrong is I don't lust after anybody much.

PUCK What an admission for a big girl!

HELENA Couldn't someone pause long enough to . . . teach one?

PUCK (remembering why he stayed by her, and also changing the subject)

They're crying out for gin in there.

HELENA  Who's crying out for gin? (irritated). I hate the stuff and Mummy doesn't drink. Not since her divorce from Daddy came through. Before that, yes, she drank, but no more than most. And she cried all the time too. I think she was miserable. Dear knows why? It's not as if divorce had ever happened to her before. I mean nobody was accusing her of being a failure. She seems to have got over it. Daddy married money the second time. I tell Mummy when she's blue that he probably did it for the sake of the business. It could be true. We have a higher standard of living now. Daddy was never mean. Unfaithful yes, but generous with money. Who wants gin?

PUCK  Titania does. She never brings any of course. The gift she brings is herself.

HELENA  I like her. She's fun. Any little Changeling Boy these days?

PUCK  You handed your telephone to him. Titania is generous too. She will let her Changeling Boy carry anyone's telephone free of charge.

HELENA  And Oberon?

PUCK  Don't you see anybody when you're on the phone.

HELENA  I saw Bottom as the Ass. (laugh). And I saw you.

PUCK  Who needs the head of an Ass in order to be noticed? And don't say it's because I wear one all the time. I'm nobody's fool.

HELENA  No-one would suspect you of being a fool!

PUCK  Suspect worse things about yourself, fair Helena than anyone would give you credit for and you are invulnerable against opinion even if you've still to cope with life.

HELENA (impressed)  That's clever.

PUCK  And yet regret from time to time that you're no Fool! That's not clever but it's wise. There — I bring to you sayings and all free of charge. And I bring you myself, a man of mystery!

HELENA (impressed again)  Mystery is very attractive. As is a manly self-confidence.

PUCK (cold suddenly)  Not in me. In me it's off-putting. Behind my back you'd call it arrogance.

HELENA  I don't talk behind a person's back (Puck laughs). Well not more than other people do.

PUCK (changing tone again — he's acting Puck after all, playing it quixotic).

Oberon tonight, I hear, came on ahead, but he arrived some minutes after his Titania did. They've been doing it for years. Phoning each other and (high voice) "Getting on my wra-aap".

HELENA (deep voice) "I've just this moment called a cab."

PUCK  Outwitting one another so as not to be the one who seems to wait. Waiting, for either of them, is un-endurable. I left them working out how it happened this time. Oberon triumphant. Titania taking to the bottle quick. Next week Oberon has the Changeling Boy, Titania says, as if she cared! He can pick the boy up from here — it's all arranged.

HELENA (a bit afraid of Puck's having so Got Into the Part). You talk as if Oberon and Titania and the Boy were really here.

PUCK  They are. In the wink of a bat's blind eye.

HELENA  You sound as if you might be Puck. Here today. In my mother's little plot of lawn.

PUCK  A little imagination. A little . . . nerve, if you, like me, call things by several names and not one of them interchangeable.

HELENA  You do not sound . . . yourself. I mean it. You are enlarged.

PUCK (triumphant) That was the idea. (leaps as Puck might). What we are tired of was precisely the t.v. naturalism . . . that low-keyed mode, like always being caught in carpet slippers with egg on your shirt front. That "being ourselves."

HELENA (reacting now a bit against his self-confidence) What's wrong with that? It's honest!

PUCK (laughs) The truth about what is "honest" is in some doubt.

HELENA Too clever for me by far!

PUCK And should I be ashamed of that?

You assume it's my fault if I crow over your head!

HELENA You are not crowing over my head!

PUCK (interrupts to carry on his thesis) One thing we are not. Not when we are at — yes let's risk a ridiculous phrase — not when we are at our "truest and best." We are not in carpet slippers then. Get under the behaviour of any man and he will crow. Take the skin of good manners off a man and he will give.

What are we usually doing but parrotting a pretty rotten part! We don't know it, but we do suspect. Things happen without reference to us. To make our part our part speak it out loud!

HELENA (thinking he's really referring to acting itself) I gave acting up. It had already said goodbye to me.

PUCK (nasty to goad her) You are a literal-minded little thing.

HELENA (answered) If I don't understand you, don't assume that is my fault. It may be you are afraid to be understood.

PUCK (calm again) Push you, fair Helena, and even you will act up for yourself.

HELENA (relieved) You were joking!

PUCK (despising her again) Let us therefore kiss and make it up.

(But he turns and walks quite a distance away)
(Mercifully the dancing procession wends through again)
TITANIA, very regal and beautiful manages to enter a
little apart from the rest, as befits what she hopes is
her "star" personality).
TITANIA (waiting for the right moment to speak her
first line).
We came to find out about the gin. (to Puck) (to Helena)
My dear, you're looking very like yourself.
HELENA  It's the best I could do in the time.

(Puck laughs)

TITANIA (to retrieve from Helena's line having made
Puck laugh) Helena is witty tonight. In a manner of
speaking.
(regaining her good humour at Puck's laugh)
Have you seen my dear little Changeling Boy of the
moment? Last time I saw him he was walking around
carrying a telephone.
(OBERON breaks off from the vanishing procession and
stands regally where no-one will crowd him so that he
may be seen, glorious as he is).
Oberon (Titania acknowledges him with a glorious smile)
My Oberon will have him all next week. We decided to
make a settlement. It only needs a little give and take
and lo, we have the world a better place!
OBERON  Not that the transformation is yet complete!
TITANIA  Well, no, in the Larger matters (she
acknowledges Oberon's grasp of the Larger matters,
with a sweep of her arm, which gratifies him, as she
intends it to do) perhaps not.

But things take time That's all they take, I'm sure. At
least we have a little give and take, Oberon and I. If
Winter comes can Spring be far behind? That must mean
something. It can't just mean that nobody cares very

much about anything at all as long as they have central
heating throughout. Can it? A higher standard of living
is a great gain. Where is the gin?

(Someone appears with bottle and glasses.

Titania needs no glass.)

PUCK Titania my only goddess, once spirit of the rich
earth, where is your glass?

TITANIA Where it ever is — here in my hand, tied with
a silver ribbon to my wrist. You might call it a leash. At
a party, I never let my glass get away, whatever happens
to my man.

(Puck pours) You love. You're Puck I'd have known
you anywhere. You magic thing. (generous) Give
Oberon a ickie dinkie too. He's been so good.

OBERON (trying to retain his dignity after that)
I am capable Titania, of pouring out a ickie dinkie for
myself.

OBERON (Now getting revenge on someone) Nor
should you trust Robin. He is masquerading as my
servant still, no doubt, and is of course a very good
fellow.

(Hoped for a laugh at the pun on Robin's name, but alas
nobody notices it).

There has been, nevertheless, a revolution, even in my
Kingdom of the Irrational, as they call it now, taking all
the poetry away and much of the sense! Puck might
dope your drink, Titania, he might dope anybody's
drink, if he were just a tiny bit more bored than usual.
That is how things go now. Don't trust Puck, my dove.
Puck no longer waits for my orders. (He's annoyed).
If there is mischief to be done, he's two moves ahead.

PUCK (mock humble). It is what you learn quickest,
master, as an underling. (bows)

HELENA (standing up, as hostess, for whoever is
"down"). Yet his idea that we take our character right

away from the play. Even just to make being someone else an excuse to see who we are. If we are . . . at all! It does sound dangerous, I admit that. But really what good can come without risk?

PUCK  Bravo!

HELENA (encouraged and excited out of her own unhappiness). And it's a party. It's not as if a party is like life! Oh, I don't know if I mean that. . . .

PUCK  Don't take it back!

For usually a party is just as boring as every day. And (yawns) this one is as likely to come to nothing as all parties do.

TITANIA (a little suspicious, but not much afraid. She is full, herself, of creative energy, and feels 'the equal' of what she recognises as destructive in Puck). These little games we all have to play to keep out of the clutches of the games that others would make us play — at parties. But (brightening) I don't mind what games you all play tonight, if there's no blood shed.

PUCK  It's a promise.

TITANIA (giving her blessing)  Then, as long as I am kept well plied with ickie dinkies of this sort, continue!

PUCK (not wanting any 'blessing') What a young soak you turned out to be, Titania, once goddess!

(A little pause. Everyone knows that Titania can
answer for herself)

TITANIA (having found her Reason)  I am over 300 — maybe three thousand years of age. Preserved in beauty of course.

OBERON  As ever, fair!

PUCK  Master of the compliment!

TITANIA (ignoring Puck and beaming upon Oberon) And yet I am still expected to be interested in a little Changeling Boy, when Changeling Boys, as we all know, are multiplying all over the place.

PUCK  Not multiplying dear.

TITANIA  There are wars and orphans. Orphans and wars. These haven't stopped, senseless as everyone individually knows they are. No glory left. Not there at least! Wouldn't you take to drink?

PUCK  (has to admire a good recovery)  So art thou justified!

OBERON  (piqued however — he likes Wars). There are wars that are glorious still. You are in your feminine way, so pedestrian after all. That's not truth — that's just reading the newspapers.

TITANIA  It does not feel as if it is just reading the newspapers. It hurts. Does reading the newspapers hurt, Robin?

(Puck is now to be enlisted as ally.

She must have an ally.)

PUCK  Hardly ever, or we couldn't do it every day. I am very good at reading the newspapers. I do it in preparation for when I'm rich.

TITANIA  You see! Puck agrees with me and he's very good at reading the newspapers.

PUCK  Nobody better.

It keeps me from boredom. But I wouldn't say that is the same as that it hurts.

TITANIA  (to OBERON)  You are angry because I am depressed and you are even angrier because I admit it. If an incessant dignified cheerfulness is what Helena wants at her parties, then she should not invite into her garden — however small and without even a lily pond or bower — she should not invite me. But she did invite me.

HELENA  (feeling guilty)  Let's all go in. . . .

TITANIA  Either out or in, a character of at least 300 years old is feeling every minute of her age.

(explains)  Have you read my notices just recently?

Have there been any for you to read?

HELENA You see it isn't possible to update the character without the play. They Noel Coward it. Or Oscar Wilde! They're actors!

PUCK It's all right. It's beautiful, Eh, Oberon. What have you got to say?

OBERON (glad of a cue) We are all characters of 300 years old, I say. And older. Some of us I dare say are immortals.

PUCK And it shows!

OBERON (takes it as a deserved compliment) I think it is because of the rhetoric that one prefers the stage, even if the money is not there. It is as if one were trying to be heard over the years, and one were not ashamed to admit it.

HELENA I like that!

TITANIA What makes me sick is everyone is supposed to be dying to assume immortality. But here I am at three thousand years old at least and I would give my life to die at the end.

OBERON I suggest that you exaggerate to make a telling phrase.

PUCK What she'd like is nearly to die at the end.

OBERON And recover in time to receive the telegrams of regret and smell the flowers.

TITANIA (refusing to be laughed at) I really am a tragic actress underneath. It's what I've always wanted to be. As Nietsche said — or somebody with a German name like that — it is the fact of our mortality that stretches life's subtlety and importance. But even in the few death scenes there are in these trite days, they never let me play in one! But if it were someone else's death! My timing of a line is not right for it. I weep all wrong, they say. If I burst into tears, I get applause. It is the way I handle a handkerchief. I doubt (in maudlin tears) if anyone has the least idea how sad that is.

OBERON (recognising the symptoms. Ready to assist her to her exit). I'll get you a little something else. It is the gin.

TITANIA For all I've had, how can it be the gin? Couldn't you just admit that I'm inspired?

OBERON I expect you had a little before we came. (He knows her.)

TITANIA (being led away) I am always being miscast as an Immortal. It is because I am the picture of good health. But I'm a martyr really. A bag of nerves.

OBERON We don't want to know, dear.

TITANIA I'm sorry. Have I succeeded in spoiling the party?

OBERON Yes, you have.

HELENA No, not really, dear. It's early days.

OBERON (but he knows how to deal with this) No, she has spoiled the party. No-one else could have done it in the time. That takes talent. She knows that.

TITANIA (giggles) I am in one of my 'funny' moods. But don't laugh at me.

PUCK (yawns) Nobody is very much amused.

TITANIA (giggles) I know. It's terrible. I'm so ashamed.

(TITANIA AND OBERON exit. Titania is not a bit ashamed. It was a Scene and she made the most of it. She knows as an actress that, as long as it's a Scene it doesn't matter whether it is pleasurable or painful, it will do.)

PUCK At least she risks it!

HELENA (worried however. Her party's not a Success) It's not going to work out. Everyone's being themselves all the time. What do you think? Should I put on some of the more respectable Pops? I've got a John Peel broadcast taped. And lovely poems in it. It really swung.

PUCK No, let it ride.

HELENA But it's not . . . fun. Not gentle either. Sort of savage . . . and worse, serious!

PUCK The least little wound and you, timid souls, you run to get an ambulance. Don't you see it's living while it bleeds.

HELENA As a child, they said, if you got scratched by a thorn, that a little blood . . . yes . . .

PUCK Let the poison out! It's there! Be sure of that. It's in the air. It's in the oxygen. The human race has lived a long, long time. And not on fairy tales!

HELENA But at a party!

PUCK Incident makes a party. What did you hope for? A look at some record sleeves? Some sandwiches and noise?

HELENA Actors at a party. It's a sort of double take. A sort of slow motion jag.

PUCK Clever girl!

HELENA (encouraged) But they're desperate.

PUCK (suggesting why) Like you've forgotten your lines.

HELENA Or they're waiting for the last trump and yet they know they've gone a little deaf.

PUCK But, if you've forgotten your lines — what?

HELENA There's always the prompt!

PUCK Right! And if the last trump sounds tomorrow?

HELENA Well . . . you'll have four minutes to get yourself All Set. And at least you'll go out with a bang!

PUCK And, my God — excuse the false hope in the expression — who says it might not be a relief?

HELENA (coming back to sense) No It shouldn't be that!

PUCK (shrugs) What it is is that at a party — and to help it is in fancy dress! — you are a character but you have no play. Or if you feel you've been just lately cast in a play, everyone else is waiting for other cues than you can now give.

HELENA  They're from another play. Not just another play, but another sort of play altogether!

PUCK  And nobody is At Home.

HELENA  That's it! (She's happy. She's "learned something and that's a joy in itself. She's radiant. Then shy.) Don't sit there, adding me up.

I'm shy.

PUCK  I'm interested.

Feel something. Feel anything.

I want to know HOW. I want to Learn.

   (HELENA in sympathy tries to take his hands.
     He drops his arms.)

PUCK  I don't like to . . . touch.

 (They are standing aware of what lies behind Puck's
  exaggerated need for "intellectual" excitement.
 Helena is as embarrassed as Puck would be if he could
    be even that. At a loss. Silent.)

 (Mercifully, the parade, minus Titania, makes its
 way across. This time it is BOTTOM who takes the star
    Spot. HELENA and PUCK Exit.)

BOTTOM  (in his Asses Head)  Nobody's talking about me. But does that matter? If nobody's talking about you, why not start a rumour about yourself?

  (He's counting the people in the front row
 or around the front circle, if the stage is surrounded
    on two or three sides)

Mmhm. Could be worse. At least I can recognise a few of my own kin here.

What kept me?

Don't ask. It would only embarrass you. But I'll tell you just the same.

It took me all my time!

Getting on and off the bus, with my Head.

Can't you just see?

I asked for a half fare. Kidding them along. What harm
in that? We all pay through the nose anyway. Could you
tell what age I was, missus? Neither could they. Except,
just at the crucial moment, my voice slipped. So then I
tried doddering a little (does that — limping around)
Pretending I was an Old Age Pensioner. Oh not just your
ordinary man in the street Old Age Pensioner. Strapping
fellows most of them. Should be doing a good day's
work. Just lounging around all day — drinking it all.
Drinking it all up. But no, I was doing a really advanced
O.A.P. One so old he'd lost his birth certificate.
Probably they hadn't begun with birth certificates when
he was born. A really old chap. Hee Haw. I was so good
at it, I expected they'd slow the bus down to a crawl,
not to rattle me. But did they? You must be joking,
missus. They made it go faster. They did. I swear they
bloody did. "You haven't a bloody permit" says they.
Says I "There's women and children here, so control
that tongue'.. "Your permit please" says they. I tried
flattering them — "You know the rules anyway." No
good. No good, missus. "Ah", says I "you wouldn't
expect a Silly Ass like me to remember his permit
though, would you?" It was great. It was developing
into a heated argument. People on my side. People on
theirs. I thought they'd be trying out their new riotous
behaviour alarm. I did. But they didn't!

We were one big squabbling family because of me. I
don't think they realised how I drew them together
starting something like that. It could have been a dull
journey but for me. And yet it would be happy in the
end. Do you think they were grateful?

"Keep all that for Charities Day," says they. "Had
anyone seen my mother lately?" I asked them next. "I
have a couple of very personal questions I want to ask

her." One women with two kids got up and left. The
children yelled "It isn't our stop yet, Mum". She was
scared I'd do her kids an injury! I never would, I like
kids. I've been a kid myself. That's why I got on the bus
wearing my head. Anyway I couldn't get a poke big
enough. Lady, have you got a poke big enough? Then
the Inspector got on and I got off. Decent chap, raised
his hat and called me Madam. He's quite used to sights
like me — obviously an experienced Inspector of buses.
The thing that didn't happen though was this — Nobody
said "That animal should be taken upstairs." A disappointment that. I like travelling on top.
Excuse me now. I've got an appointment with some oats.
Hee Haw. Hee Haw.
   (Exit BOTTOM. His turn should be something like
        a Clown's between the acts in a circus.
    Sort of On and knocking his pan out and then off.)
        (HELENA and PUCK are midly amused)
HELENA (remembering she's hostess). Food! That
little girl who played the Lion is dealing with the
business of food, not that there's much to do. Every-
thing is orderable. Except people should enjoy them-
selves.
PUCK To provide for people to enjoy themselves!
That's the last thing you could prepare for.
HELENA I'm sad suddenly. I'm poor company. Sorry.
PUCK There are people in unlighted corners in pairs.
Demetrius — whom you seek — might be among them.
HELENA That wouldn't be a consolation to me. Any-
way I've looked. I'd know the costume. I once played
opposite it — remember? Before I gave it up for a
Steady Job.
PUCK You need to work?
HELENA Don't you?
PUCK To live, I mean.

HELENA  I can't live on my father's immoral earnings always. It's not considered decent now not to do something, even if you could just lie around.

PUCK  Who would just lie around? There are lots of things to be done — If you don't have to make money at it, you might make your living at it.

(he's bored because Helena understands about
nothing he says)

I'll go on in.

HELENA  (calling after him)  In 300 years it will still be Demetrius. Is that awfully out of date?

PUCK  In 300 years it will still be Helena.

HELENA  But it won't be me!

PUCK  It might not even be Demetrius. If humanity goes, there might still stand a quiet building where they housed the First and Second and subsequent Folios and all the books from all the centuries before this one. Does that console you?

HELENA  It doesn't. Should it?

PUCK  It makes me laugh. But I admit that's not the same as being happy.

(They both leave, but not together)
(EXIT PUCK and HELENA. The lights dim.
Some of the characters — Bottom and the
Changeling Boy and the girl who plays the Lion —
come on and move stage furniture so that we know,
just sufficiently, that we are no longer in the garden
but are indoors. They laugh at Bottom trying to carry
something. And despatch him.

CHANGELING BOY  You've got enough to carry with that head.

BOTTOM  Wanted to help.

LION  We'll manage. But thanks.

(Exit BOTTOM)

CHANGELING BOY  Someone put the gin bottle in

the wrong place tonight.
LION   Maybe it was me.
CHANGELING BOY   Don't just automatically take the blame.
LION   Sorry.
CHANGELING BOY   It could have been me, you know.
(They are happy, working together. It is not because of anything inside, but because they are working together. that they're content).
(He's found a paper with writing). Is this yours. (Lion looks and shakes her head. She's busy with things.
LION   What does it say?
The writing's . . . difficult.
CHANGELING BOY   I am trying to catch a star — it says. I'd catch a bus easier. You may say I'd get there more certainly catching a bus. Or on my feet. I thank you for your concern for my danger. You intend it kind, and I apologise that you don't understand me yet. And yet it seems to me I must try to fly now, or else I'd see myself as too heavy a pedestrian. I'd limp even before I'd travelled a long way on your plane. If I fly, I'll fall, but it will teach me a little how to walk.
        (They look at each other with a smile that says
    "It means nothing does it? They crinkle the paper up.
LION   Don't ask about it. It might embarrass whoever wrote it. It's some sort of admission so I don't think we were meant to have seen it.
    (They have gone and come back to examine what set
        they have arranged — very little, just enough.
        A rug perhaps to indicate indoors. And stools.)
OBERON   (enters) I wonder what you think of the gimmicky idea of the producer who cast a girl to play the Lion.
CHANGELING BOY   It isn't for me to say.
    (Oberon makes him stay near him for the rest of the
                    scene)

LION  I was glad. But I don't know why.

OBERON  Why in the theatre more than any place does gimmickry find its feet, so to speak?

LION  I usually get the stage to sweep.

(Changeling Boy nods "And me")

OBERON  I think there's a very simple explanation.

LION  Is there? I suppose they didn't have enough men . . . who would . . . just for a few lines . . . maybe.

OBERON  My dear, if you can't be humble enough to take a part because it has "only a few lines" then you're not humble enough to act at all.

(As he says this, he also illustrates the contradiction —
of how Proud also is the business of being an actor)

HELENA enters again)

HELENA  Perhaps you were glad to get a part at all?

LION  I was. Yes. I'd do anything.

OBERON  My point was that gimmickry is the bed-fellow of stagecraft because there is something perverse in anyone who works at his life this way.

LION  I don't see that. I think it's a fine way to work . . . at your life.

HELENA  Being Helena sort of allows me to describe myself. I'm the kind of girl for whom there always is a Demetrius who "got away". There have been others who'd have stayed, but I'd rather there had just been Demetrius.

LION  I think that's nice.

HELENA  But oh to be Hermia with a sort of queue and to be calling out "You'll have to take your turn."

LION  I wouldn't like saying No.

OBERON  There are ways girls have — Titania should be here to illustrate — ways of stalling you, ways of never having to say No, so you follow like a tame lapdog, convinced that one day there is something you can do that will elicit a joyous Yes.

(He has said too much. PUCK should be here.
      He'd have welcomed the exposure.)

HELENA  You're a funny choice to play a Lion.

LION  He wasn't supposed to frighten people.

OBERON  Excuse me, that was just Shakespeare's irony.

LION  (surprised)  I didn't see it like that.

It's fun to roar quite loudly when everyone knows it isn't a lion at all. I mean it's good because it's Just a Play.

OBERON  There are those among us who eat and sleep what you call Just a Play!

LION  Of course! You see, the kids at home -- my brothers and sisters, there's quite a bunch of us, they love it when I roar in this. (her costume).

      (She demonstrates. They smile)

OBERON  For you it really is makebelieve.

LION  (happily)  Oh yes! Life at home is not like it at all.

OBERON  Titania there, now sleeping it soundly off, you'd think an earthquake shook her when she's in a part. And to emerge again, it is very near to being physical pain.

(change of tone) Alas! It is impossible to live with her. It's sad of course. But one really must — one has one's own Art! — there has to be someone who will . . . listen. Titania is always listening to herself. And when you are talking what she is waiting for is her cue. One loves . . . but one cannot live with that.

      (He's said too much again.)

HELENA  The reason I gave it up was that it was frightening.

OBERON  Doing without it would be more frightening, to me.

HELENA  The inference that one "plays many parts" and not just from youth to age, but simultaneously. I

didn't know who I was. All I did know was that I was
. . . in flux.

OBERON  Because one hopes one has a little . . . talent,
one escapes being . . . a criminal.

LION  And isn't that wonderful?

OBERON  Yet it is never my play I'm in. Some day I
tell myself it will be my play. But maybe it won't ever
be. But without the . . . accident . . . blessing? . . . that I
act, it is as if there is such energy in me and it is there
specifically to say No to all things as they are. No. No.
It won't do! It isn't good enough. No. No.

(At the point where OBERON is defining what the
Energy he is conscious of is there for Puck enters,
unseen by others but seen by the audience.)
(PUCK has entered and is listening.)

PUCK  (as if at a cue)  Yes, master?

OBERON  (on cue immediately)
"My gentle Puck, come hither. Thou rememberest
Since once I sat upon a promontory,
And heard a mermaid on a dolphin's back
Uttering such dulcet and harmonious breath
That the rude sea grew civil at her song
And certain stars shot madly from their spheres
To hear the sea-maid's music."

PUCK  (gently, but transformed)  I remember.

OBERON  "That very time I saw, but thou could'st not,
Flying between the cold moon and the earth,
Cupid all arm'd; a certain aim he took
At a fair vestal throned by the west,
And loosed his love-shaft smartly from his bow,
As it should pierce a hundred thousand hearts;"

(knowing he 'has' them, but testing them too)
Shall I go on?

LION GIRL  (in near whispers)  Please!

HELENA  Oh Yes!

OBERON (refreshed for their encouragement, adding power)
"It fell upon a little western flower,
Before milk-white, now purple with love's wound,
And maidens call it love-in-idleness.
        (PUCK, completely in character alert, happy,
                moves near)
Fetch me that flower; the herb I shew'd thee once
The juice of it on sleeping eye-lids laid
Will make or man or woman madly dote
Upon the next live creature that it sees.
Fetch me this herb; and be thou here again
Ere the leviathan can swim a league."
PUCK (all energy now, as if winding himself up to move with the words)
"I'll put a girdle round about the earth in forty minutes.
        (Only he doesn't move. He stands 'carried away'.)
OBERON (as the man, no longer Oberon, but still transformed).
Is it the language? Need one ask? It is certainly the language. But that's gone. It hangs with . . . nostalgia now. Something from the past.
PUCK From a past so far away that it has become fiction and therefore still. We can believe it. Did anyone ever speak like that? Nobody now speaks like it, not even to himself!
LION GIRL (shy) I speak like that to myself . . . sometimes. If there is nothing else for it. Oh not like that really of course. I don't have the vocabulary. I have to use the words I use to order my mother's groceries in. But it mustn't be in the same tone. I am explaining badly, but I mean it must carry much more weight.
HELENA How can you sort of say . . . anything in these days, with everything sort of against you . . . except in a sort of quotes.

LION GIRL (delighted) But that's how you do say it! In a sort of quotes. But not, as far as I know actually ... quoting from ... anybody. I'm not very educated I mean. So I haven't got anything to ... quote from, except of course what everybody else ... has and hears and maybe stores away in forgetfulness. Oh, I mean I don't know how to say the things I very nearly ... know but I can't get any nearer to it ... unless I try to say ... something ... even if it's only to say that it can't be said ... by me ... yet.

OBERON How did it come about that you found your foot on any stage for things on stage are said Out Loud. You speak ... I mean it would suit you to speak ... in a whisper so that the words would drift away and not leave a mark.

LION Yes! That's what I'd like. Not to be having to say anything at all. Because I don't ... know about anything.

I sweep floors well. I watch rehearsals. I like actors ... at work.

HELENA I see through you! Puck, I'm getting clever!
PUCK Don't blame me!
HELENA But look at her, she's doing the female thing. She's trying to please. By her modesty.
LION (surprised and interested) Am I? Maybe I am!
OBERON Modesty is pleasing. Why shouldn't it be? But you're too apologetic. Stand your ground.
LION Yes, I should. My ... tentativeness ... it makes people uneasy. And she may be right. It could be a release she's offering me. I have to entertain other people's ideas about myself, especially if I don't welcome them. Anyway it's a way ... maybe to grow.
HELENA (generously) You win.
LION Oh no, I don't. You're right. Modesty is 'pleasing'. What I hope, to balance that, is that the fact

that it doesn't always please but sometimes irritates
... forgive me.
HELENA   Don't grind me under your heel.
LION   I occupy this ... skin ... Maybe I roar a little
bit.
HELENA   (tired of the subject). I expect people are
beginning to feel empty. I am. I think I'll investigate in
the kitchen.
LION   (this explains why she's been invited at all)
I left everything out the way you said. In case I've done
anything wrong, shall I come?
HELENA   (suddenly aware of how little she herself has
done to prepare for her guests).
Of course you needn't come. It's all very simple.
(exit HELENA)
PUCK   (direct)  Does she pay you to wash up?
LION   Papier mache plates? No.
PUCK   Why get hidden away in the kitchen?
LION   A person in a kitchen isn't hidden away. Of
course you don't see them unless you're there too.
OBERON   We stand chastened.
PUCK   I don't. If she was in the kitchen, she liked it
there.
LION   It's true I don't deserve to be pitied for it.
PUCK   Ah master (mock bow to Oberon) you stand not
chastened but accused of pity.
OBERON   Accused?
PUCK   Only if you are looking down are you in a place
where pity is profitable.
LION   If to you pity seems like condescension, it seems
to me it acts like kindness.
OBERON   Your gentle roaring is not without effect,
child.
PUCK   Doesn't being Put Upon matter? It should. You
could be cherishing a hidden ressentiment. Don't be

Put Upon. It's bad for the character. (He pronounces ressentiment in French. It's a straight lift from Nietzsche "The Will to Power.")

LION  Who's being Put Upon?

For one thing I got fed before anyone except Bottom. He found his head gave him special conditions matching my own. We ate first. Together.

PUCK  And so you learn how to be two moves ahead. You take advantage of your disadvantages. It's the slave complex.

LION  Haven't you ever worked in a kitchen?

PUCK  I eat in restaurants where strangers are. I am happier where there are strangers. They never assume they know you. They know they haven't had time.

LION  My mother's face when she's cooked up something nice — especially when she's done it on the cheap — you'd think she'd painted something. We eat it in a few minutes. She doesn't mind. No-one will be putting it, up for sale decades later under the auctioneer's hammer, but she's made something. She knows she has. It's enough.

PUCK  It isn't enough.

LION  You're right. She has to see our faces enjoying it.

PUCK  And so it isn't just a therapeutic exercise!

OBERON  When a woman has a child, that is the supreme moment. That's the time when they have created and know it. That's their object d'art.

LION  I've seen my mother in childbirth. I was fourteen. That isn't how it is. She hadn't "created" anything. The baby was suddenly and terribly and beautifully there. My mother had nothing to do with it . . . except experience the pain. And the relief. But my mother knows, as she holds the little strange . . . event, that it was not her. She holds the child . . . in trust . . . or something. It's my father who knows he has . . . created

Us. Not my mother.

(quite strongly) My mother sees herself as an instrument. She very nearly doesn't see herself at all. I love my mother . . . because I pity her. Since I was fourteen years old. I can't see myself like that. I can't see anybody like that except her.

OBERON (embarrassed, changing the subject slightly) You have a large family?

LION (laughs) Six of us. Seven soon.

PUCK Very irresponsible! (half joking)

LION (joking too) I'm thinking of having my mother and father certified. They seem to enjoy it.

PUCK (hastily) Not unusual, they tell me.

LION They enjoy children. My father is as much a child . . . younger in many ways than me.

PUCK Your mother is not.

(wondering how he knows, because it's true)

LION I can't guess what's in it for her . . . now.

PUCK I bet you can't!

OBERON Don't badger the girl!

LION (to Puck) You really want to know, don't you?

PUCK I want to know everything.

LION (almost cruelly, reacting to the 'evil' thing in Puck's insatiable curiosity).
The second of my brothers — he's eleven years old. He won't grow up. He's remained at the age of 4.

(PUCK reacts with gratified greed)

PUCK (to himself really) It's happened.
(It's the moment of extremity he needs.
It's more than "chat".)

LION I think . . . maybe in a way it's all right.

PUCK Nonsense. It's a blasphemy.

LION (defending what she needs to know about) It's true it's only my mother who knows it's all right.

I only . . . hope.

OBERON  The sentimentality of the average mother of course will come to her aid.

LION  (feeling trapped by two people whom she doesn't expect to understand).

She's very practical about it.

PUCK  (sarcastic)  She lives with "the problem".

LION  I don't think we're any of us sentimental about it.

PUCK  Sentimentality is something that needs distance to lend enchantment.

LION  That I understand. I don't understand everything you say. Whose side you're on . . . I don't. . . .

PUCK  Do you boast about your brother for instance?

LION  (nearly crying in anguish)  No, I can't.

PUCK  (goading her on)  I bet you can't.

LION  It took me ten years if you must know. . . .

PUCK  Yes, I must know
    (She looks at him trying to understand why he seems
        to enjoy hurting her, not understanding anything
            except that she is hurt and it must continue)

LION  To tell a stranger (Like you, she means)
my mother's got a sort of faith or something about it.

OBERON  (piously)  She goes to church.

LION  No, not any more. She doesn't go to church or anything. (sarcastic) She has a lot to do, of course, even on Sundays.

OBERON  (still trying to put things right) Your mother of course needs to . . . believe . . . needs to find 'for herself, that is, that everything's really . . . all right.

LION  (angry with him too) Yes, she does. She needs to find for herself . . . Yes, she does. You don't find anything much, unless you need it.

PUCK  But what she doesn't need is sentimentality!

LION  (calmer a little)  When my father realised what

he'd . . . fathered . . . he. . . .
OBERON (embarrassed, very much embarrassed by
now). Well a thing like that, to a man, is always a shock,
of course.
LION  (to show of what stuff is her "family")
My mother tried to pretend he wasn't — my father
wasn't . . . the father.
PUCK (delighted)  Bloody brilliant!
LION  (quite strong)  Is that sentimental — would you
say?
    (She's searching desperately for a handkerchief.
          But she's not crying.)
OBERON (offers a handkerchief)  She roars, the little
lion.
LION  (ashamed, trying to laugh, not to continue to
embarrass them).
Only in . . . a good cause . . . I hope. But it could be
pride . . . I know.
PUCK (determined to go on 'exposing' something)
What did your father say then . . . about being . . . a
cuckold?
LION  (looks straight at him)  He didn't believe her.
He knew it wasn't true.
OBERON  Very touching.
LION  (to Puck)    And because she was willing to let
him think so, rather than that he should feel destroyed
by worse, he loves my brother who's four instead of
eleven years old. He loves him maybe the best. You
wouldn't understand a thing like that.
PUCK I'd like to understand. I'd like to understand
that
 (he turns away, sharpens up again almost immediately)
more than I'd even like . . . another drink.
    The CHANGELING BOY has brought bottle.
    Glasses are at hand. PUCK insists on pouring.)

PUCK (to LION GIRL) Will you . . . partake?

LION Thank you.

> (Everyone is there suddenly — the procession —
> except TITANIA, who, one presumes is still
> sleeping it off.
>
> BOTTOM walks round looking at everybody.
> Holding up a mirror to faces on stage and in audience
> alike. Only PUCK does not flinch from his image.
> He stares at it as if it disgusts him.
> LION girl turns shyly from the mirror,
> not wanting to be seen too clearly
> just at that moment.)

HELENA I was thinking of that very amusing play about a similar subject. It had a great popular success. In theatrical terms — that it not popular of course with those people who never see the inside of a theatre between one pantomime and the next.

PUCK (jeering once more, at Helena this time). The Common Herd!

HELENA I would vote Labour of course if I voted at all. One just does not see any difference. Of course one is aware that difference there is — somewhere.

OBERON (He's glad to be talking about something safe, a "play").

Very bitterly funny it was, that play. It caught on marvellously. It was just what people needed of course to be able to laugh at. Very bitter laughter it was of course.

PUCK The refuge of the damned is in bitter laughter. Had you heard that?

HELENA Not . . . recently . . . no. (She says that as if it's a film she's missed.)

LION My mother never goes to the theatre. The seats are expensive.

HELENA (snobbish again). There is television.

LION We don't have it yet. I'm looking forward to it, but it would keep (laughs) some of our lot off their studying. It's a small house — for a family like ours! (She's happier).

OBERON (snobbish too) It's not a play you'd see on the box of course. People have a long way to go yet.

LION Maybe it was cowardice, but I didn't go.

OBERON Beautifully done. I'd have been interested in your opinion.

LION My mother thinks our brother is . . . a sort of . . . gift.

HELENA Oh Lord! No!

LION She thinks we must have done something . . . good in order to deserve him. Even if we don't seem marvellous, she says, we must have been considered Strong enough. He strengthens us, our brother, she says.

PUCK Just who "considered" who "strong enough" if she doesn't go to church.

LION She used to go.

PUCK Does she go around crying Hosanna all day long.

LION On the contrary. (She isn't going to explain).

PUCK On the contrary — what? (Now, he must know. He's hoping for something now).

LION It will seem like a contradiction.

PUCK (very excited) I am at home in contradictions!

LION My mother only seems to find things to say at all when you can see by her face that she's been crying all night — when my dad's on shifts.

OBERON I want your opinion though. It seems to me a highly original idea. To take such a subject and have us rolling in the aisles. Really one could say no less than that all these areas nowadays can be made monstrously funny after all.

HELENA The acting needs to be superb. It was a London company. I mean they said so. Such a compliment.

OBERON  It was adequately acted. Let us say the acting was adequate.

HELENA  What one was doing in spite of one's ... perhaps reluctance ... was laugh.

PUCK  (laughs) Air a problem, exercise it, walk it round the block — or rather parade it.

OBERON  Nothing but good can come of it. Sweep it under the carpet on the other hand, as I suppose you would!

PUCK  Would I?

> (Everybody knows he would not.
> So there's silence)

PUCK  (to everyone exept Lion Girl)  Weren't you just relieved that these characters could laugh? Didn't it help you to sleep more comfortably in your bed?

OBERON  What's wrong with that?

HELENA  It ran to packed houses in the Metropolis.

OBERON  On Broadway.

HELENA  It's being translated into French.

OBERON  It's to tour Russia.

PUCK  There are people everywhere who like to sleep at nights. In spite of anything at all! So do I!

OBERON  It was highly praised. Only a single voice here and there, with a doubt or two. But an undoubted talent, they all said.

HELENA  A lecturer once gave a weekend school on how perhaps the only way to deal with the darker subjects nowadays is to make people laugh them off ... I think he said.

PUCK  They're making a musical on Auschwitz next year. Hadn't you heard?

OBERON  (confidently) The times are out of joint!

PUCK  (triumphing over Oberon's having spoken up as if inspired in spite of himself for his own argument). Oh cursed spite, that ever who was born to set it right?

OBERON (stunned) Hamlet. The Prince. Act . . .
Scene . . .
PUCK Let him collect himself. He'll tell you the
number of the line.
LION (who has been getting something different from
all this than PUCK was getting).
You all know where to find such comforting things.
PUCK (surprised) What comfort's in that.
LION That someone said it. Is that silly?
HELENA It doesn't change the facts.
LION Of course it doesn't change . . . the facts. But
when there are facts that . . . trouble you, I don't think
what you want is to laugh. I think maybe what you
want is to be able to cry.
(to Oberon) when you were speaking the lines from the
Dream a little while ago, it was beautiful. I was glad. It
seemed enough, just for that moment, that it was
beautiful. I couldn't say Thank you at the time. It
would have made a fuss It would have spoiled it.
PUCK By thanking someone, you take a share of the
credit.
LION (really interested at his theory) Is that so? And
yet it feels more that you don't know who to thank.
Maybe all you can do is choose whoever's there . . . or
something of the sort. But honestly I just don't know.
       (Her 'modesty' is real, it silences everybody
                    for a second)
OBERON I have made a silly ass of myself, child.
BOTTOM (on the scene,once again). Hee Haw. Don't
boast. I do it all the time.
OBERON (with dignity) At least I won't make it worse
by apologising.
HELENA "If we offend . . . it is with our goodwill.
OBERON That you should think, we come not to
offend."

BOTTOM   Everyone gets in on the act. Act Five. Scene One.

LION   (smiling at him)   You have such tender ears, Mister Ass.

BOTTOM   (bowing)   Your servant Mistress Lion.

LION   (grateful to get the chance to clown) Your servant, Mister Ass.

BOTTOM   Servant Ma'am.

LION   Servant suh.

BOTTOM   Ma'am. (bowing and scraping)

LION   Suh.

> (It is almost a comic ballet between them
> for the moment.)

BOTTOM   We rustics, ma'am.

LION   We little scullery maids, suh.

BOTTOM   Any bowing and scraping to be done, I'm your man, ma'am.

LION   (happily)   Any little jobs in the kitchen, suh, and I'm your girl!

> (They're joyful and have — we hope —
> changed the mood all round.
> HELENA is, however, beginning to recognise
> in the ASS someone else.)

HELENA   Madam Lion, who is your . . . friend?

LION   (who knows who he is)   He is the Ass with the prettiest ears I've met this day.

HELENA   Under those ears, is he Demetrius by any chance?

BOTTOM   (running) Anybody who is really, some-what permanently interested can soon find out.

> (HELENA runs after him, joyfully, perhaps even
> comically — not afraid to make a fool of herself by
> hoisting up her long skirts and showing legs as she
> makes off after him.)
> (Enter TITANIA well rested and rather surprised at

the "spectacle" HELENA is making of herself, running after "a man".)

TITANIA (Then sees OBERON looking handsome and the CHANGELING BOY looking very nice indeed. Sleep does knit up the ravelled sleeve of something or other, it's true.)
That Changeling Boy really was worth a little quarrelling over, my Lord. I see that now.

OBERON (very charming) Madam, he suits you very well.

TITANIA No, you keep him with you. Show him beautiful things. It is your week. But, after all, I'll be very glad to see him again.

CHANGELING BOY (speaking up for himself) If you can, both of you, spare me, there is a telephone to answer about now, and if I do not answer it, who will? If that is Demetrius and I believe it is, he who was, before that, our Ass, Helena may not be hearing the telephone, which, I know, is about to ring.

OBERON Then don't wait for it boy. Go answer it.
(It rings.)

TITANIA (as Changeling Boy runs out) It may even be the B.B.C. with a tiny part for someone in the Borderers.

OBERON A fine, swashbuckling exercise!

TITANIA Just made for you, my dear.
And now, whom do we say our elegant thank you to? I have to make my exit. Where is Helena? I had a lovely little snooze and everything has changed. I feel quite renewed. Sap begins to flow. And hope is possible.
(Enter Helena and Demetrius, detached from his Asses head, a good-looking young man.)

TITANIA (to Helena) Ah, you got him, dear, better luck this time.

HELENA Hippolyta has been on the phone.

DEMETRIUS   She will not come. She apologises too.

TITANIA   I never could stand her, dear.

No real temperament. And yet I don't know! To phone at the end of a party and say No I will not come, it shows a flair!

HELENA   It was not that she had washed her hair that kept her from us — although she had.

TITANIA   She rinses it but it shows dark at the roots.

DEMETRIUS   No-one, it seems, had invited King Theseus.

PUCK   In these days, he is a character not so much superfluous — which he's not! — but incredible! . . . which he is!

OBERON   What is Theseus's loss is Oberon's gain.

TITANIA   No-one is fool enough not to believe in you, my Love.

PUCK   The irrational forces are everywhere. And obvious.

TITANIA   Puck is so precise. But in his way dependable. If he says he'll circle the earth in three-quarters of an hour, that's what he does.

PUCK   Oh would that everything were half as easy!

TITANIA   My dear, you just don't have a romantic sense. Now Oberon — he is quite different.

OBERON   I could almost suggest we set up house together again?

TITANIA   Oh Oberon you are asking for a miracle.

OBERON   True!

TITANIA   Little tricks you can perform, but miracles — now admit it — they're out of your range. It's better that you come to tea on Tuesdays, and Fridays, as you always have, for supper. But what else did Hippolyta say, Demetrius? The more I think of it the more I envy her the panache to phone at the end and say she will not come.

And yet how can one use the device oneself? She'll have told everybody that is what one will do, and so it can't be done! Such a pity though. But what did she say? As her real, everyday excuse — and none of your symbols please.

DEMETRIUS   She said she was neither young enough nor quite old enough yet, to be seen at a party without a man. She said that people would talk.

TITANIA   Why yes! What a good idea! One will talk. One must get one's own back. Are our taxis on their way, dear Oberon? Now we are so close to each other again.

OBERON   Yours has promised to come first.

TITANIA   I forgive you everything, darling!

CHANGELING BOY   Titania's car!

TITANIA   (to Demetrius)   Any time you — and Helena are having a little shindig again, need I remind you both to remember me? If Oberon's not free. I think I may say quite confidently still, that I can avail myself of a man to fill the bill, (waving). Lovely, my dears. See you Tuesday, Oberon. Be a bit late. So that I may be ready for your arrival.

OBERON   (to Demetrius and Helena — who are joint hosts now). I think I, on the other hand, shall not wait for a car. The night air is very pleasing, especially a few hours before the night's at an end. I shall not beg you to invite me again. I am there. I don't expect you to forget me.

(Exit Oberon, having upstaged Titania by not asking
to be invited back.) Come, boy.

(The Changeling Boy, goes with a
wink back to those left.)

PUCK   (tiring at last)   In   our   meeting, what   has changed? Nothing!

LION  GIRL   (carrying the glasses out. Picking up

      things) Oh everything! (She's gone out)

PUCK  But for how long?

DEMETRIUS   What you want is Insurance cover man! (Demetrius and Helena go out, holding hands.)

PUCK  (to audience)

No-one has changed.

But nothing is quite the same.

I wanted something else.

But maybe what I got is enough.  (He bows.)

THE  HARD  CASE

by

JOAN  URE

# THE HARD CASE
## a monologue

On Saturday, 2 January 1971 a crowd of
80,000 football fans watched a match at
Ibrox, Glasgow, between arch-rivals Celtic
and Rangers. The match ended 1—1 with both
teams scoring in the last minute of play. Fans
who were heading towards the exits rushed
back to see what was happening, and in the
resulting crush, sixty-six fans were killed and
one hundred and forty-five injured.

Scene: Something between a Courtroom and
a Music-Hall.

Time
    Some weeks after the tragedy at Ibrox Park.

THOMSON: Good evening, Ladies and Gentlemen. The name is: John Allardyce MacFie Thomson. Native as they say, to these parts. More or less.

That is, I occasionally feel responsible ... not often ... never, in fact, if I can get away without ... but now and ... beginning.

Ah, thought you had me there, officer! Thought you'd be able to take me down in your notebook and thus as it were tidy me away.

Keep me off the streets.

Ah, I am not saying I can explain any of it. Just the same the reason I did not plead Not Guilty ... although who could exactly blame ... the reason ... I would not be fobbed off ... wanted the full treatment was ... in order to be publicly aired ... (As if he smells bad!)

Judge, I know that it is not easy, a job such as yours is, that only through a deep sense of responsibility to the community, would a thoughtful man like yourself take it on. I know it's not just because of the sense of importance. I know that the wig is weighty, the robes no sinecure. I know all that. Over the years, I have not been slow, sir, not slow to have pity for the likes of you all who have to bear the burden of a seat on the bench in judgement over your fellows. Many a time it was I

myself, minister, reverend, Mr. McGeachie, I who said,
"I'd shut them away . . . at least for a lifetime". That's
the sort of thing I was amongst the first to coin a phrase
with.

So I am not without sympathy with your position. Not
without.

And although almost overcome with the Honour, I also
know you aren't overendowed with time. I am not the
last to realise how you stand there. For death looks us
all in the face. Ladies and gentlemen of the jury. Not
the first nor yet the last, not the last whose finger has
been raised in anger, whose nostrils have wrinkled in
scorn, whose arm has been outstretched in blame. I have
done all that sort of thing, so I don't know that I have
any right. To ask you to give me a chance. To speak up
and not just for mys. . . .

There have been many poor buggers, there will be many
many more, who have stood in the dock — stood at the
penitence stool even and nobody ever thought There
but for the grace. . . . Many poor buggers before me.
And when given the chance they hadn't a word . . . so
why I?

Yes, your worship, I will try to guard my tongue. At
the same time, I feel that it's all got to come out. Now
or ne. . . I may be using language advisedly even. The
only language for the job. I suggest that only a certain
amount of foulness is here going to let in the daylight.
Something very like it anyway. A sort of rape of the
lughole. I wouldn't have always said so. I have altered a
few of my opinions about a lot of things . . . I'm
afraid.

The vileness is not in the language . . . not in the
language all by itself. If it's there in the streets, it's
maybe necessary. We are Uptight here, so much of the
time.

Meantime I am trying to reach you. Trying to get to you where your honour must live.

... But your honour, it can't be done (having a laugh at the imaginary Judge he's haranguing, when he's not haranguing someone else). Just keeping to the bare facts. No facts are (chuckle) as bare as they seem. Not just like a baby's bottom. And there again (a chuckle) there again ... you could hardly call that decent ... every minute of the day or night.

Anyhow the copper gave you the facts. You have got all the facts! Written down. A lot of good it seems to have done you!

(He dons policeman's cap and assumes persona
of policeman.)

On the morning of 3rd January of the present year the defendant was proceeding, no he was more wending his merry ... no, weary I'd have described it, world weary his way seemed to be although it was but 10.30 a.m. and they were not even Open ... anyway it was the Sabbath. You call it a Sunday, I expect, my Lord. Stepped out as if he saw nobody. Stepped in front of car pulling away from the kerb, an accelerating vehicle, the shilling in the parking meter having been spent. Leapt back, the defendant, as if he'd been bitten by a Skye terrier. Very sharp teeth and I should know. Brought up with the brutes in the kitchen.

Then with his umbrella on 3rd January with his umbrella at Copland and Lye's big side windows, banged, battered as if with a rapier, poked at the glass and banged in Wellington Street by the side entrance and thereby broke the glass. Shattered and scattered. A piece of glass was embedded in my skipped bunnet. In my hat your honour, and it narrowly avoided my face. I might have been scarred. My blood might have flowed into that gutter. For life. Scarred. Either P.C. Macdonald or I myself that is, we were equidistant from the scene of the immediate crime and we might have been marked for the rest of our lives, either of us — him as well as me and neither of us married men yet, even. Spoiling our prospects in fact.

So P.C. Macdonald and I had no alternative — we were already without sleep for 48 hours — we were by no means at our most tolerant. Later we felt we had to acknowledge the fault in our possible behaviour. That is, your honour we did not feel inclined to let the defendant get off scot free, as they say who should know better for we are not that sort of race at all. Very little is free.

I mean we realised that if we had just given the man a bit of a shake such was our mood that we might have dislodged the man's head. And we could not but have regretted that, later.

That is, we were on edge, a bit edgy, on edge. It had been — you'll remember — quite an evening of it. Quite a night to forget. Yes.

He also gave us some trouble. Had to be forcibly held although his hand was quite badly cut.

A piece of glass got into the defendant's hand, yes your honour. We had to charge him first then take him to the Infirmary. No your honour, we had to take him first to the Infirmary and charge him thereafter. And as you may remember, your honour, hospital staffs all over the city . . . in fact all the forces of law and order, healing and help were under more than normal strain. Even the ministers of the church were busy. The defendant had to be held down on the table, sir, held down, while they put six . . . eight . . . something between six and eight stitches in the defendant's hand. It took 4 members of staff and Macdonald and me. Already overworked. And fifteen minutes. Without even a whiff of an anaesthetic. It turned my stomach green. Green, my lord.

Perhaps I got that wrong, but I think it not unlikely. There wouldn't be much anaesthetic left perhaps. Well perhaps it wasn't without anaesthetic at all. I wasn't myself feeling well.

Thank you, your honour. I will take a seat. Thank you your honour. (reassuming role as defendant).

Yes, madam, the mark is almost away. I doubt if you could see it. I must thank the surgeon. A credit to our long history of skill in the sciences, in medicine especially. Also I must apologise to him. I must have caused him pain.

(As if to Judge)  No sir I do not wish to plead now that I have been punished enough. I do not feel absolutely certain that I have been punished enough.

But I do not want to go to prison. I doubt if that would help.

And a fine can pay for nothing at all. Money is no way out, I mean. I mean I could probably afford the fine. But what about any poor sod who couldn't afford it? Who hadn't got the cash. He would have to go to prison, I may presume, having got so far. Not that I know nearly enough about the workings of justice. Maybe he'd have been discharged . . . by now.

Not that I am qualified to know yet.

About anything, my Lord.

I have become suspicious, for instance, of the usefulness beyond the bed and board stage, the usefulness of money. (chuckles, shrewd) Not that it isn't useful! Everything can be abused. But money as a way to distinguish one man's crime from another? I have come so far my lord, I have come so far and I doubt if breaking a plate glass window was what I'd call a "crime" at all . . . not when you compare it. . . . It may sometimes

be a necessary protest . . . a means of expression . . .
because nobody is listening to what you say. I've seen
these black power guys on the telly. I think I know
what they mean.
I did it, sir, I think I did it, because I did not know what
to say, your honour. What to say . . . to be understood.
To say.
My political history? Ah there you have me. (chuckle)
I've got none. No political history at all. Have not
cast my vote even in the Municipal — (chuckle again) —
perhaps particularly not in the Municipal for who —
just answer me that one — who does give a load of
manure for what happens in the Municipal? And yet . . .
maybe it's about . . . time? Don't know. Can't attend to
everything. Got my — had my own little concern . . .
dependant on the wheels continuing much as before . . .
dependant on the state of things as they are . . .
dependant.
I voted once after I got demobbed. Then I don't know
— I suppose I wanted to feel what it would be like to
feel I was pulling my weight in affairs beyond my
window box. Small garden in front, in fact. Decent, if
narrow, terrace house. In Hyndland.
Too young before I joined up. Couldn't wait. Thought it
would all be over before I was of age. But made it. So
can count myself . . . an officer . . . and a gentleman . . .
a soldier for a short time . . . and everywhere was the
front line. Like now . . . perhaps . . . no . . . not quite
. . . perhaps like now.
Hyndland is a safe seat for our chaps. Our member's
wife and my wife Betty once had their picture in the
centre section of the Glasgow Herald — the woman's
page it was then — now you have to be more tactful
(chuckle). You mustn't call any page . . . the "woman's
page" any more in case you seem to be referring to the

Little Woman. The photo was taken in front of the tombola stand. Betty was behind it. The member's wife was making the compulsory purchase. Quite right of course, quite right. If you believe in something, you support it — if you've got the time. That is Betty after we got the washing machine and the waste disposal unit — the waste disposal unit, my lord — it saves you walking up to the bin — Betty used to help at the coffee mornings. She always bought the milk. Did her bit for us both. In that sphere. As good, they said, as half a dozen voters. I don't know. She borrowed the car too — I didn't mind, she's a careful driver women aren't really all they say as drivers, careful on the whole — when the literature at the election time had to be taken from door to door. Betty had the right kind of trusting smile, they said. That pleased her. I paid — I used to pay for the petrol. Letting them use my car when you've just had a new set of retreads . . . that sort of generous gesture . . . it's not to be sneezed at, my lord.

(Slumps, tired.)

I was nourished by notions like yon.

To think how long I went getting nourishment like a life-raft from notions like yon! I don't know what I'll do now. Am afraid.

I'm trying to make it brief. It's not a brief matter. It's almost a summation of my whole life.

My life, your honour. This 'ere is My Life!

Forty-seven years old. Given every chance by good, respectable parents. Glasgow High School for boys. No less. Elmbank Street, I hear the bell as I . . . even yet. Almost two highers, and got two lowers. No University. Had enough. Father's little concern. Quite good enough for me. Not a greedy man. I believe that's true, in its way too. Never wanted two cars or house at the coast for the hols. (Change tone.) I was sitting there in the stand. Safe because I had a few bob more for a seat. As simple as that, the difference. At the end of the game. A draw. No hurry. Take my time. Not really watching the southwest end of the terracing. Not really watching. Then . . . the shambles . . . And because I paid more for my seat I was . . . spared! Folk died a park's width away. And it isn't the same on T.V. It bloody isn't. I couldn't get it out of mind. You see.

I couldn't help feeling I'd pushed them. Some fourteen years old. I hadn't moved. I hadn't pushed them. But I thought it was me, I was sure it was me. Ridiculous? .Maybe.

Except I didn't know what I'd done what was really so wrong. Except that they were crushed, mangled. And I . . . wasn't even scratched.

Where did the difference lie? They died. I survived. Weans not long out of diapers. Dead. And Jock Thamson lingers on!

(Angry) Lingers? No. I've given up . . . ma . . . lingering on. Changed! Changed. See me. Not the same. And lost my best girl to prove it! See me. A man on his own. For the first . . . the first bloody time in my life.

And I don't like it.

I wish it had never happened. I wish it would go away.

Me . . . yer actual Glasgow Hamlet! I bet you thought it was someone else, lady. Bet you never thought he'd look like this. Bet you thought he'd be all in black . . . (sexy throat noise) with tights you have to soak to get into. But that's the view you had, miss? Holding one hand to the head and the other hand covering quite a (dirty laugh) lot that matters.

(Serious) I'll never wear black again. Not even an arm band. The world I live in needs . . . colour. The world I inhabit needs play. (funny now) Bring the colour back to your cheeks, lady? Give each cheek a little pinch for

you, will I? Well if you're shy with me or if you find me
undesirable, as the saying goes, turn to the right or left
and see what you'll get yourself into. (end of dirty
laugh session again.)
(Serious) They played rugby at the High School. My
mother didn't encourage that. And my father had gone
to a free school just run by the Corporation of Glasgow.
Just a Good School it was. At Bellahouston. And he was
a football fan like everyone else. Rugby is really not our
game . . . not our gem at all. My father took me . . .
began to take me to Ibrox as a boy. Football's a Great
game. I still think football's a great game. There's
nothing wrong with football! But I couldn't get to sleep
that night. My wife Betty — she was still with me then —
it wasn't till later she — she's a kind woman — I've been
making her life a hell — her life too, a hell — tried that
fatal night after the "tragedy" tried to force one of her
sleeping tablets in a little milk down my . . . my
thrapple . . . as if I were a wee wean. None of that, I
said. I have never in the whole course of my existence
actually buried myself from experience — not even with
an aspirin — it's just that I seemed to juke it . . . somehow . . . seemed to escape without any medical
assistance. Not even when I had flu . . . in '57 when they
called it Asian (chuckle) so it would go away, I suppose!
And leave us our (ho ho) Arian island . . . as if ho ho
we'd ever have made it all by ourselves.' (a sound like a
sob . . . that's nowhere to tears yet.)
Wha's like us? Aw wha's like us. Gey few . . . and (he's
almost yelling in his pain.) . . . and they're aw deid. . . .
(Softly) How to mourn . . . their passing? How to
mourn the years that are awa' . . . and not before time!
Ayee, ayee, ayee.
(Suddenly businesslike) We don't have yer actual
wailing wall in Glasgow. I think it's about time it was

built. There's a big grey wall up at Barlinnie . . . before
they even open up the gate . . . something along these
lines would do, I thought, the moment I saw it . . .
very tall and grey and terrible — it would do to be going
on with. I'll propose it to the City Fathers. Save on
available cash too. That sort of thrift is not to be
sneezed at, either. Why build yer actual wailing wall.
When you've got one . . . all the time up the back of
Maryhill. It's only the barracks that they pulled down.
The prison — as you can see, lady — the prison is still
Essential. There might be other men . . . even worse
than me! For don't think we lack yer actual gangsters.
Don't think we have to import your actual bad men. A
couple — you may remember the case — got tried during
the week of official mourning — two of our gangsters —
who needs fiction? — our fact is too much for us, ma'am
— that's why, that's why, that's why — our facts don't
come predigested. Our gangsters are only safe as long as
they stay in the States. The same week . . . as if we
needed a sort of underlining . . . as if there would never
be an end to the evidence against us . . . two gangsters
were tried for entering Stobhill — Stobhill Hospital —
and trying their bloody damndest to shoot to kill a vital
witness.
Oh God those men must have been desperate!
Oh God. Oh God. Oh God. What is it like in prison, then,
for year after year after year after year? I do not . . .
dare . . . to find out. Dare not.
But . . . the . . . vital witness . . . was not dead, ladies
and gentlemen. The vital witness . . . escaped. . . .
Maybe the vital witness . . . is, in some way, oh I'd like
to think so — I think I need to think so — the vital
witness . . . is bloody . . . immortal. Maybe . . . the vital
witness . . . canny . . . can't be killed. (Very quiet, very
fearful — a little hopeful perhaps, but not sure of course,
not quite sure).

No your honour, she is not in the court this afternoon. Perhaps if you sent me to prison, she might return, for she is not a hardhearted woman and if I appeared to her to be quite friendless, I know she could not keep away. Women are like that. Women are — thank God — like that, occasionally. I think I only have to say I'm sorry . . . and (chuckle) . . .

But, if I may explain Betty's behaviour, it is partly because I have somewhat altered my own. Never did drink before. Only a tot at the New Year, and then only among friends. Such an exhibition as I "make of myself" — as she quite naturally puts it, leaving it open that I am making some sort of choice — it's never happened in her family before. (chuckles) In fact I never thought to be glad I'd lost both my father and mother. Never thought to get some comfort from that thought. But it comforts me. And I admit it. But Betty's mother is still . . . alive . . . very much (chuckles) very much as a matter of fact. No wonder Mr. Wallace copped it. In his shoes, I'd have been glad of an early "release". But Mrs. Wallace put pressure on Betty, I think.

Even so, she wouldn't have gone. Your honour.

(Taking a breath, before the punch line) It was the T.V. cameras and catching her in her curlers. Imagine how she felt, my lord. For the first time . . . on the telly . . . and without even a scarf to cover the curlers up.

Never before. Even in bed, I never did see Betty without her scarf over her curlers. Even in front of me and we'd been married — 25 years it would have been in July — she thinks I don't remember these things (chuckle) but I only let on that I don't. (chuckle) She remembers enough for both of us! As a sort of ammunition, I sometimes think. "John our Wedding Anniversary was on Friday. Not that I can expect you to remember . . . after all these years, I suppose." (chuckles tenderly).

She's a nice woman, Betty. I shouldn't have subjected her to being seen like yon. And it wasn't my idea. Of course. Even the cameramen were only doing their job. A way to get a touch of humour into the news — Betty done up in her curlers caught on the hop, opening the front door, thinking it was just the kids pulling the front door bell — from the high flats, as usual. Cameramen are human. Nerves all shot to hell like anyone else. Needing a touch of humour to cool it a bit for them to bear. Betty had to pay the piper. Necessary. Necessary sacrifice? I don't know. And not a life and death matter.

At a certain deadline, on the edge before the pain pounces . . . there is no place to go away from tears . . . no place but the belly laugh.

I too needed a way to cool it. A way to cool it down. For presentation. Playing it "heartless" . . . till the heart is at room temperature again. Both space and time . . . I needed. To discard the uncontrollable irrational anger . . . the need to apportion blame to somebody . . . living.

I knew I must not be quick to act in anger. A plate glass window or two. What's that . . . (Feeling in his trousers for money) I could have paid on the spot. Knew I mustn't get off scot free though.

Enough of that. Give tomorrow's Scotsmen a break. I found myself saying aloud. I found I was walking around talking aloud. No-one . . . precisely . . . was . . . seemed to be there to talk to about anything that mattered. (unfolds newspaper).

The Glasgow Herald for Monday, January 11, 1971: "The television cameras could not capture it. Poignant moments. The silences between the hymns, the sobbing of the women. For once prejudices . . . forgotten . . . all denominations . . . represented . . . young men who played their game for their living had attended the funerals of the innocent all that week . . . had experienced more sorrow than many people meet in a lifetime." Unquote. Unquote. (folds newspaper).

Young men. A crowd of mainly young men.

(dons judge's wig and robes)

I have tried the case set before me against my will.

Given the matter some thought.

The man's whose case we have been trying, ladies and gentlemen of the jury, went on without giving it much thought.

Yet we have the man's word — and in a way we may trust him if not for the facts, at least for the way of getting it Said — that he noted the death of the innocents and felt personally bereft.

Perhaps football has been carrying something foreign to it as a sport altogether. It raised the gate money but at what cost. For religion was too much for a game to have to carry. It's time to see that both sides are shooting their goals for God.

We can learn as much. Maybe. I won't myself, walk in any Orange March again. I give my testimony. I may continue to like the good tunes. But suggest the tunes be taken over (smiles) by something like the Salvation Army. With a wee bit change in the words.

Our . . . the defendant . . . I suggest his wife forgive him. If there are reporters in the court, I suggest it be suggested to his wife — if let me see — if Mrs. Wallace, the mother-in-law reads any newspaper at all — that in that newspaper some mention should be made to the fact that it is not the most terrible thing that ever happened to anybody to be photographed with curlers in. At the same time I suggest that T.V. photographers be a bit more sensitive. I would hate it to happen to me.

And I believe, I plead — I the judge in this court go on record, as Pleading for the man whose case, by fair means or foul — one can't be sure — but whose case he insisted on Being Continued until the issues had been, as he might have put it although he didn't, been inspected under the light.

What he seemed to want was that it Be Recorded. That nothing that was important be lost.

We may deprecate his manners. In fact, I personally felt it . . . it could hardly be distinguished from a deliberate contempt of court. It's been a hard case. I suggest to you, ladies and gentlemen of the jury, that we be bound over, if necessary together, to preserve the peace . . . not the peace for the sake of the quick snooze . . . but peace with greater justice.

Now, if you will stand I will, as is my custom, rise and quit the court. We may shake hands in the vestibule some day . . . we may even sip from the selfsame cup of tea. I take three lumps, with lemon.

# TAKE YOUR OLD RIB BACK, THEN

by

## JOAN URE

# TAKE YOUR OLD RIB BACK, THEN

Characters

MALCOLM PATERSON, about 28 years of age. FIONA McROBERT, younger.

Place: The St. James's Centre, Edinburgh.

Time

Festival time in Edinburgh 1974.

(Speech begins even as Malcolm and Fiona enter, Malcolm pulling a pushcar behind him and holding an unattached microphone before him as if to catch sounds from the audience or the imaginary people in The St. James's Arcade already.)

MALCOLM    We agreed that we would spend the Festival here. Here beside St. Andrew's Bus Station, and inside this, the St. James's Centre. Seeing why people come here, or don't come, to such an artificially constructed complex.
I have my microphone with me to interview passersby. Oh shut up, Virginia! Not that she's uttering a sound, the little one, but it does not look too good to be pushing a child around and enjoying it.
Fiona, here, my young and very talented wife, hopes to get inspiration, or at least a little reinforcement for her instinct that she was doing the right thing for all three of us when we moved out to live in the countryside. There are no Iced Lolly temptations there, for child or adult, and a constant reminder that we are not far from our ... roots in the earth, and, if necessary even in our knees cultivating with difficulty the soil from which we have sprung.

I have, of course, to commute to the city, but I cycle to the bus stop five miles from our cottage, and on the bus it's only a two hour journey — little more — and very interesting Pentland hill scenery and pleasant passengers. I am a University lecturer. Termtime coming up means that I shall carry young Virginia here on my back in one of those papooselike affairs. But my back is strong and straight, and the students will take turns to heat her bottles or open the small tins of concentrated nourishing food. By that time, she'll be off the breast. Fiona must not be distracted. My wife is an artist! I am her personal, private patron. The students and I intend to include little Virginia there in a class-project. Country-dwelling is best, but we also like the best of both worlds. Edinburgh is the capital, so we owe it to ourselves to know what's what there. However, we have to keep hens somewhere; it is not possible in Rose Street. It is also our duty to grow a bit of seakale: it is a doublepurpose vegetable.

FIONA   We cannot both work at once . . . ever. I am not working here. I am here on holiday, at the Centre. But Malcolm is, of course, hard at work.

When I refer to work of course, I do not refer to hens or seakale. For other people, they may be work for us they are a healing diversion, for which we never-the-less take some credit. We are, both of us, (gloriously smiling) terrifically intellectual and not at all ashamed of it, although we know it is fashionable now to despise the intellect. (laughing a little) And we do indulge in that of course, to keep things in perspective. We are enthusiasts. Malcolm, here, is a tower of manly strength, so he can afford to push Virginia about in the pram everywhere. To demonstrate that he accepts a role in changing the image of the manly function. Malcolm insists on being my husband. I insist, however, that I do not own

anybody and therefore the idea that I "have" a husband
is against my principles. Marriage is really too easy, isn't
it? But I don't wear a wedding ring and that is a demonstration almost as good as the real thing.

MALCOLM    Fiona revels in the unconventional. I am
not Stuffy either!

FIONA    (turns from audience to Malcolm)    You,
Malcolm, are a typical sociologist. You are a lecturer to
students for a living. Heaven help them of course if they
believe that passing exams can possibly measure
knowledge. You revel in all this around us. It gives you
so much to disapprove of. It is a typical street scene, but
artificially constructed. It was not healthily allowed to
grow, shop upon shop. The implication is that you can
get everything here. Though the building itself is a
monstrosity. The only buildings in Edinburgh that are
beautiful, except by accident, are the Banks: they even
floodlight some of them in the dark. Odd priorities they
have in Edinburgh.

But here Malcolm, you have a typical sociologist's
dream. You are a parasite upon people and their
reactions. Typical you are of the person who believes
objectivity comes through analytical thought and a tape
recorder. Whereas it is a gift of . . . grace. You thrive
upon other people's mistakes too. If they didn't make
mistakes, you would be out of business . . . like the
police.

MALCOLM    My role requires patience. And study.

FIONA    You are a patient man. And a scholar.

MALCOLM    An academic, not so much living as
roosting in the groves of academe. Fiona, a former
student, became my duty. I will not rest in objectivity. I
hesitate to call Fiona a project. But sometimes I believe
she is my cross.

FIONA    Of course you are not typically typical. You

are Unique to me. Even when I was your student, you were an individual unique to me.

MALCOLM  Fiona never wanted an alternative to University. She had me, she said, and that was enough. (aside)  What I notice, however, when we go out on my projects together is that I cease to take notice of other people, except as they encroach upon ourselves. I guess that is one of the dangers of the nuclear family. Sufficient in itself as it seems to be.

FIONA  But you are a lecturer, with a degree and a position and a regular income — for which I'm grateful because it lets me do what I do just for Love with nothing sordid about it connected with money and killing all romance. He has an audience of younger men and girls too; that is very stimulating for him. They depend upon his appearance of scholarship. He keeps just a little ahead, telling them the books to read just after he's read them and before he's quite forgotten the gist. There is also a regular stream of ideas thrown at him, which he can pinch and incorporate in his thesis. He is really in the best place for him, with a little observation of places like . . . like . . . this, ugh, on the side. He has to keep in mind that what actually exists of course are his books and his taperecorder. He is more or less interchangeable, ten a penny. His microphone there is more creative than he is. I do not tell him this unless he's inclined to throw at me that it is he, not I, who brings in the wage packet. I have learned something from my mother's technique. She used to tell my father what the economic rate would be if housewives were paid . . . and my father couldn't have earned as much, even working overtime. It gave my mother great strength of character, knowing what she was worth; it gave her the balance of power, knowing that she would never get anything more than just the housekeeping.

MALCOLM   It is no wonder that I fight for the rights of women's liberation. Fiona's old man would be off the hook, if her old lady got paid. But it will take some time to convince the Common Man of all that, of course. We cannot expect them to be quick on the uptake without the educational benefits some of us aspired to.

FIONA   It's great for Malcolm at the University too. He comes home many a night, having pinched a brilliant idea for his thesis from a student and having convinced the student that it was old hat. It is, however, and he admits it, only because he is an authority and marks exam papers that he has an audience at all. Whereas I . . . I, well I (all vitality) I improvise. Without authority. Sheer will power, in fact. I mark nobody's exam papers, so nobody needs to be nice to me.

MALCOLM   With your need to be . . . frank, it is not easy.

FIONA   Oh yes, I know that, and I praise you for it. You notice how I praise you for it, don't you? With me dancing along, it must make you feel, often, such a pedestrian. But we all have our functions, do we not? Now is the time of the girls, dear. The best the men can do is . . . help. I am on the razor's edge of selfdiscovery. I follow the promptings of my conscience and neither commerce nor convention will divert me.

MALCOLM   Making a spectacle of yourself . . . to see if you're real.

FIONA   (aside)   To give the game away, we do not really observe what goes on in St. James's Centre. (giggles)   We are here to see if St. James's Centre will be stimulated to any sort of response at what goes on in Us. I am a cartoonist/poet. It is part of my technique to put on a . . . performance.

MALCOLM   You are an embarrassment, that's what you are. I could do my job unobserved; it would be a lot more comfortable. Connected with your ideas of what is right, however, it is Me that gives myself away, and what I get on tape is . . . in spite of that. It is not normal sociologist's selfeffacing technique. It is also very exhausting sometimes. Sometimes we have to take to our heels, when, occasionally, a wheel comes off the pram. Imagine the confusion, avoiding a massacre.

Sometimes I think the old ways are better. Often the only voices on tape I have at the day's end are Hers and Mine! And Virginia's if she cries. Shut up Virginia! It's useful having a baby too young to understand you; you can use her a bit like kicking the dog, only she doesn't know it. Shut up, Virginia, and lie still. There is, of course, not a sound out of her. An aspirin in the morning gripe water is . . . effective. Don't tell Fiona that however. She might increase the dose.

Fiona, however, is the real embarrassment. I say that to your face, Fiona. And I mean it.

FIONA    It pleases people, Malcolm, when other people behave outrageously. It saves them from having to do it. When you shout at Virginia — oh don't think I didn't notice — it makes every mother and child cling close together. Cruel parents are awfully good for welding healthy families together. I am here — not you, because you are really just a taperecorder — but I am here demonstrating that, if women around me spend half the day rocking the cradle while on their lap is a bowl of peas for shelling, it isn't because they have no choice but do that. They have. Except they are aware that babies need comfort and that people would go hungry without shelled peas.

MALCOLM    To everyone his . . . tasks. Her tasks, I mean. We were not sent into this world to be on perpetual holidays. But to make a holy day of work.

FIONA    However, at this moment, I do have my sense

of obligation. People who come in here out of the rain
for a look at the shops are bored. Or else it's the East
wind they're here to escape from. They will not have
enough money for what they want, and yet they're
tempted; the devil has been at work dressing the
windows, so they will buy something that they will
grow tired of before they've got it home. It'll all turn
out to be a terrible cheat. So it is my duty to stop them
spending their money on things they don't really need.
It is my duty — since I know better — to interfere in
other people's lives. It's all I'm good for actually. Food
— I'll allow that. They really must eat. And it's not their
fault that half the cost goes into the packaging. To save
on wages. However, curtains and furnishings. Are out.
Knicknacks and gnomes. Green ladies and fuckling
ducklings. Broody hens and wally dugs.

MALCOLM    Fiona, there's a woman already taking
notes.

FIONA    Good.

Garments here are not to cover nakedness. Who need be
ashamed of nakedness anyway. All our bodies, even
yours sir, are beautiful. These garments here are because
we are really ashamed of a nakedness that is spiritual.
And when I say "we" of course, it is only a euphemism.
I really mean You.

MALCOLM    Fiona, you are becoming rather . . . rude.

FIONA    Provocative, dear — not rude.

MALCOLM    (to people supposed to be passing)
She sees it as her duty to entertain and instruct . . . free
. . . to give you all, and me too, and little Virginia,
something else to think about than the glamour of the
market place.

FIONA    It is a glamour, friends, which cannot disguise
the poverty of the sodden soul.

Malcolm, I believe somebody threw a tomato.

MALCOLM    Yes.

FIONA    And tomatoes are Food. That's not the way to behave with tomatoes, Malcolm. Perhaps I have been too forthright.

MALCOLM    People don't like to be preached at, my dear. You are lucky not to have had a stool thrown at your head.

FIONA    But we could make use of a stool, Malcolm, in the cottage. A squashed tomato, however, is a waste.

MALCOLM    I know, Fiona, that your attitude of arrogance is quite deliberate.

FIONA    I am a failure, Malcolm.

MALCOLM    You choose arrogance because girls must stop being quite so charming. Quite so humble even. We know that when women in the past have put on that "how little I really know about anything, while you of course are exceedingly clever", they are cheating, making it impossible to answer you back. A tomato, dear, is an answer.

FIONA    Perhaps it was the Fuckling ducklings, then. So I succeeded! I mean I really sounded as if such words rise to my lips like regurgitated milk to the lips of a baby.

MALCOLM    People will learn that it is not at all to be taken for granted that the standards laid down by the genteel as to vocabulary . . . the vocabulary suitable to young girls from your background . . . may not be questioned.

FIONA    Is the tomato . . . quite uneatable, Malcolm? Oh, well!

MALCOLM    (calling off stage, where the tomato came from) Thank you friends. We will take home your gift and feed it to our hens.

FIONA    It is very rich in vitamins, a tomato.

MALCOLM    I think this child needs feeding.

FIONA   Which child? Oh how terrible. Is there a child in that crowd being neglected?

MALCOLM   This child.

FIONA   Oh, little Virginia. Why, I suppose so.

MALCOLM   Yes, and changed, I fancy, too.

FIONA   I intend to breastfeed little Virginia here, I think, but not till we have gathered more of a crowd. It is of course your selfappointed task to change her, to show that a man can minister, even in Scotland, to the baser needs of someone other than himself. Which my father never did.

MALCOLM   So you've got strength to go on with our demonstration?

FIONA   I think so.

MALCOLM   Pity.

FIONA   Malcolm!

MALCOLM   I hoped I might persuade you – no, put it to you, that the crowd isn't exactly on our side. I thought we might erect an umbrella, this golfing umbrella, to act as a sort of tent, as in the desert. We could put a placard on it: See inside Contemporary mother and child. That way no one is . . . forced. Don't you think that would be colourful, and a variation? Something like the circus we think we should be.

FIONA   It is one's duty to illustrate that one is not ashamed of nourishing another life at one's breast.

MALCOLM   One is just a little surprised.

FIONA   I was surprised at first. I thought I might not be able to suckle an infant at my breast, like any ordinary, untalented mother, but after the first surprise, I began (giggles) rather to enjoy it. I just wish Virginia had been twins, for aesthetic reasons. (She wriggles at the sensuous satisfaction of the idea.)

But changing the child's napkin is your job. As an example to my own father, who would not even push

the pram. Not that he's here, except in proxy. Come
Malcolm, it is thus, in these days, that one is crucified.
That shouldn't be beneath you.

MALCOLM    (after thought)  You are showing off,
Fiona. Right now, I believe you are showing off.

FIONA    You are analysing me. Don't do that.

MALCOLM    You are making no effort, for instance,
Fiona, to lower your voice. When you talk to me it
sounds as if I'm a crowd. I am your fellow conspirator,
not your slave, Fiona.

FIONA    You get your own back when you analyse me.
We are falling into the old "It's either you or me"
patterns. So stop it.

MALCOLM    Sometimes it really is either you or me!
I admit this is not a busy time in the Arcade. What
people there were when we got here appear to be con-
gregating at the far away end . . . as far away from us
as they can get.

FIONA    There is nothing wrong in organising an
audience in neat rows.

MALCOLM    But I cannot really pick up what they
are saying. Surely they are not afraid of my microphone?
No it must be you, Fiona. You terrify them. They are
used to men with microphones, from watching television
which everybody now does — except ourselves —
Surely t.v. has not queered my pitch. Surely the general
public has not wakened to the notion that being plied
with a mike and a set of leading questions is an act of
impertinence? It is an act of impertinence, of course,
and one would never have the brass neck to do it if
one wasn't being paid well for it. Just the same I don't
want them, in Edinburgh which is my daily bread, to
realise that they can organise to knock the bread and
butter out of my hand. No, they must stay to be
recorded, at least until I've finished my thesis on the

Scot and Confrontation with Authority.

Fiona! They are beginning — back there — to put us, you and me, on to film. That I won't allow. It is my job to study them. It is not their turn to study me!

FIONA    I won't raise a hand in your defence, don't worry. I know you don't want to be saved from difficulties by me.

MALCOLM    I'll just get myself this air gun! How propitious that there happens to be a Sports shop in this complex. And yes a little ammunition — oh, I see it's really a sort of dart that this gun fires. Well, that's even better. I'll be able to count the score. (Then ashamed at his enjoyment) Fiona, shouldn't you stop me? Aren't we both pacifists?

FIONA    You can't kill anybody with that. You'd only slightly maim them. Don't aim for the white of the eye, that's all.

MALCOLM    Fiona, you're provoking me to combat. Like any mediaeval lady.

FIONA    Oh, so I am!

MALCOLM    Seeing me with a gun excites you!

FIONA    So it does! Good gracious.

MALCOLM    I am patient and — yes — glad to be encouraging the New Woman in all her tortured search for identity. But not when you revert to the mediaeval . . . in the interest of your enjoyment of showing off.

FIONA    Coward.

MALCOLM    Defend you, I seem to be forced to, rather often. Yet you are continually throwing us both — and our little Virginia — into the teeth of the Enemy, the Scotsman, his wife and their belligerent brand of conservatism. Yet here is an Innocent Small Child. We ought not to experiment with our normal reactions too far.

FIONA    The only way to introduce an unpopular idea

to the Scot is to make it instantly unpopular. Then there will be a whip reaction, for reaction — not action — is the way they move.

MALCOLM    But if I have really to shoot somebody, Virginia will have at two months, a father with a criminal record.

FIONA    Virginia may benefit from your having a criminal record. We know how standards are changing, and you have no authority unless you've been to prison for what you believe in. Go right ahead and shoot.

MALCOLM    But shooting is not what we believe in!

FIONA    In the interests of what we stand for, it is called for sometimes to do things opposed to. . . .

MALCOLM    Sorry. I find it does not come naturally to me to shoot at unarmed men and there's only one person there with even a walking stick. If they pushed their womenfolk in front of them, I might feel provoked . . . it would be such a sign of the fact that they didn't believe I'd actually go and do it. But they look even a little frightened. So I can't.

FIONA    One of them was shooting at you, with his camera.

MALCOLM    It's nearly the same, but it's not the same, just the same.

FIONA    Leave the revolution to someone else . . . because of your scruples . . . because of your need to see all round a situation before you act! That's terrible.

MALCOLM    I know.

FIONA    We do not want to brandish our exemplary conduct before Virginia's opening eyes, you know that. We want her to have something to be ashamed of in us, or we will stultify her attempts at communication with us.

MALCOLM    Couldn't we risk treating a child like a child? Even like . . . your mother treats a child. Cuddling it sometimes.

FIONA    I will not treat a man like a child. Humouring him, when I think he has failed the situation's potentiality.

Anyhow, you'll be talking about mortgages next! Virginia must not get between me and my doing what I feel I want to do. You know I mustn't run the risk of turning my resentment for my frustrations upon her in my old age when she is trying her growing wings and I've just let my wings wither away. Burning her up with my envy at her daring.

Oh, and you did look like a hero from an Old Western.

MALCOLM    Did I?

FIONA    Lovely, you looked. I was really proud of you. You didn't look bourgeois one little bit . . . for that moment.

MALCOLM    I am of course in agreement. An avant-garde family environment does give a child a belief in the adventure of life, in the possibility of leaving it a bit different from the way we find it.

Spotless parents make for guilt-feelings in their children.

FIONA    (encouragingly)    You act unconventionally quite often, Malcolm.

MALCOLM    Thank you.

FIONA    It's only that I sometimes doubt if you enjoy it.

MALCOLM    (confessional)    Sometimes I want to pick up Virginia and cuddle her and tell her that she's Daddy's good little girl!

FIONA    Wow! I hope you flinch from that.

MALCOLM    And I've such an impulse to tell her that she's lovely — that she's the loveliest thing I've ever seen . . . apart from you of course, when you're at your best.

FIONA    I respect you for admitting your failures, Malcolm. If we don't admit our failures, we'll never improve.

MALCOLM    And heaven forbid that our little girl
grows up with the idea that she's expected to be a Good
girl, while other people's little boys are so obviously
going to the devil and enjoying every minute of it.

FIONA    Oh, and to think that she might believe that
she is more beautiful in your eyes than any other kid!
We are a nuclear family but we must not perpetuate
its defects.

Now it's confession time, I too must remind you how
often I have admitted that praise for anything has such
a blossoming effect upon me. And so I really have to
watch my motives for doing things. I was told, even by
my father — which is rather surprising — that I was
rather beautiful as a child.

MALCOLM    You would be!

FIONA    Malcolm! But it makes me, and you've seen
it, so terribly coy. I mean, you know how I trade upon
the fact that you find me rather pleasant to look at . . .
in my weak moments, I am even grateful for it. And you
know afterwards that I am so ashamed.

MALCOLM    We cannot be perfect all the time. We
really should not expect it of ourselves.

FIONA    It is worse, if anything, however, to have it
impressed upon us that Daddy loves us, not just out of
the richness of his Love but because we've been good!
Being good, we discover, will get us a smile. It may even
get us a sweetie, whether we have just brushed our teeth
or not! Being good will have been put in front of us as
something that it really pays us to be.

And yet it is frightening, Malcolm, how that limits one's
energies for selfdiscovery . . . in a girl, I mean. Conform-
ing we have been for generations to other people's ideas
of what makes us appear to be Good. One is really just
being Obedient, but we don't know it till it's often too
late. Virginia could be like my mother, a speechless

rebel, a mass of resentments for not occasionally being bad. Fatal. Fatal.

MALCOLM (after offering Fiona his hankie). May I confront you with an unpleasant thought?

FIONA Certainly. It's so much more constructive than an unpleasant feeling. With a feeling you just have to wait till it gets better. And our time is limited.

MALCOLM You do remember that, before you went in for the cartoon/poetry business, where there's quite a lucrative bit of loot to be made on the side, before that, you fancied going on the boards. As an actress. However, there have been no good parts for girls in plays since Ibsen, Shaw and Chekhov.

FIONA Oh, and Strindberg.

MALCOLM Yes, but none since 1956.

FIONA Agreed. The rise of the angry young man killed off the girls' parts.

MALCOLM So you said. I hadn't noticed.

FIONA But then you're not a girl.

MALCOLM Ten girls there are for every good female role and some of the girls' parts are now played by boys: it has something to do with the shortage of dressing-room space. So, as an actress, you know that even sleeping with the director wouldn't have you playing Ophelia the following season.

FIONA What is all this leading to?

MALCOLM So sometimes you are showing off. To get attention. And not on principle at all. But out of ... need.

FIONA The Leith Police dismisseth us, I see.

MALCOLM Well, we have to entertain unpleasant thoughts. Delivered as objectively and coolly as one can, of course.

FIONA And not out of any idea of revenge? Because I called you a coward then?

MALCOLM    Just entertain the idea, particularly if it caws the feet from you.

FIONA    It does. You have taken, for the moment, the dance right out of my step.

Showing off? He may be right. He may, alas, be right. It is a melancholy thought, but I will thank him for it. Thank you, Malcolm, dear, thank you.

MALCOLM    Now stop it, don't make me feel bad. Don't take it too meekly, mind. Cherishing underneath cancerous resentments.

FIONA    True, entertain it. But combat it! Yes. Make it the excuse for my . . . my monologue. Yes.

FIONA    (She uses the whole acting area for this one, striding around like a Principal Boy).

Poor Malcolm. All he has is other people. He admits that there is nowhere for the white, middleclass British male to Go. He agrees with Stanley Eveling there. The white British man has been emotionally everywhere. He is waiting for the sun to set on the last part of his empire . . . me. I am the last part of his empire. And I . . . the world is mine. When nobody has expected very much of you, it really does build up an accumulation of generations of energy. I do not even know Who I am yet! So my life is full of interest. Where I go hardly enters into it. Who I am I really do not know. I am not my mother, and that's a cert. I see it in the reluctant looks she gives me. I feel it more painfully in how she puts me down and cossets Malcolm, as if Malcolm were her son and I some stranger.

I pity my mother, and that is terrible.

I love her, and she can't love me for envy.

I do not know how much my every action is . . . reaction. How much my methods follow the Politics of being Liked. I am all Possibility. Schizophrenic. Numberless images of myself to get into perspective. So

'Seven Characters Out Of The Dream'

'The Hard Case'

that one day I will begin to see other people . . . like
Malcolm . . . and love them for their infinite variety.

Meanwhile for Malcolm, there is North Sea Oil. There is
Nationalism, and the new face of Socialism still to be
found.

MALCOLM    There is nationalisation, which is not
going to be easy, because those that Have Hold and
Hold and Hold. There is all that.

FIONA    For me, for the first time in history, there is
ME. The black in America and I — we are the only sort
worth more than cocking half an ear to . . . the only
sort the most ambitious of the sociologists find worth
following around. (chuckle) Malcolm only uses this
place and these people as an excuse. So that I won't
notice that I am his material. Malcolm's no fool.

I observe people observing me. They don't all like what
they see. And yet I'm interesting. Even to myself! Do
you know this — I find heterosexuality is devious
enough! We, the girls, we are the emergent nation
within the nation, the revolution sharing your double
bed — if you're lucky.

It's a wonderful and a frightening feeling.

It is difficult not to be boastful about it.

It is in fact not possible to Live it, without being
Boastful about it. I know why old Mohammed Ali used
to mouth around 'I am the Greatest'. You've got to, or
they won't even dare to try to knock you down. And
you have to get knocked down to find out whether
what you were standing up for was really . . . difficult.
Really strait and narrow. Honestly.

Fiona McRobert taking on all Comers. She is the
Greatest. Walk up and observe her. Better far than
Rangers and Celtic. Cheaper too. Less commercial than
the World Cup. A winner at 11.30. A knockout just
before the dawn.

Ride with McRobert, the girl without a grudge.

I don't give a grudge time to develop.

I am not going to end in a madhouse. I start there and work my way . . . out.

MALCOLM    Sometimes you so embarrass me, I don't believe I can stand you another day.

FIONA    Give me a towel: I'm wringing wet . . . like April.

Oh Malcolm. I'm where the action is. How can you resist me? Anyway, it's your job.

MALCOLM    When I'm with one of these old-fashioned, gentle girls who queue up in the corridors offering to type my notes for me, who sit there at my feet and look up at me as if every word that drops from my lips is the morning dew, sometimes then, I think I've been precipitate. How easily I could relax even with Fiona's mother.

FIONA    Oh mama is great for folk to relax with. The trouble is she's less encouraging when you're on the move. But just lie down on the couch and look defeated, and apologise for ever having aspired, and mama is a joy to be with.

MALCOLM    If she would even give her own mother a good word!

FIONA    I love her. It isn't my job to talk of her with Respect. It's yours, for you don't really care what'll happen to her if there's some day nobody around her waiting with parched lips for a cup of weak tea.

MALCOLM    There is always someone with an empty teacup.

FIONA    Do you think my mother is going to look beyond the family boundaries for her tasks?

MALCOLM    Shut up.

FIONA    I'm winding down. I'll shut up, yes. Go on.

MALCOLM    It is so alienating when she talks like that.

People don't immediately assume that you only tear people to shreds if you care for them. And of course that isn't even true. People are sometimes torn to shreds because nobody cares for them. But when I consider — turning my back on Fiona for the moment — when I consider how she has already ruined my chances of promotion, it takes all my sense of duty to carry on. I don't know what I will have to bail her out for next. I worry about what exposures she is going to resort to so as to fight the false modesty in herself. And I blush. Sometimes I blush from the tip of my nose to my navel. I doubt if I have the strength. I have to remind myself (turning to Fiona) that if she — if you have the strength, then surely I have! But that does not convince me. It's something quite . . . chemical that does. Something that may change. So I mustn't miss it. As things are just now, I only have to look at you and . . . I find it difficult to believe that you can be so ridiculous, such a fool, sometimes even so wrongheaded, and sometimes even cruel . . . without it leaving scars upon your face. And a devil's mark upon your body.

FIONA    Malcolm, stop it.

MALCOLM    No, I won't. If you weren't who you are and where and when you are, you would have been obliged to be a witch.

FIONA    An easy myth: I will have none of it.

MALCOLM    It is my presbyterian background. You are too enchanting, too powerful, for a woman: you must be a witch!

FIONA    You know that is a lie. I am just a 1970s girl. Articulate and therefore . . . harmless. I am on show and so you need not fear me.

MALCOLM    If you were alive in ancient times, with all that drive, and no chance of personal achievement, you would have had to manipulate people. As powerful women always have done.

FIONA    Then you could have called me a witch.
But the manipulator is the destroyer. She keeps the man
she learns how to anticipate and Use . . . she keeps him
as her child.

She had no other occupation once. It wasn't allowed
her. It would really be, even for me, much easier to put
all my energies behind the encouragement of other
people but then I would expect gratitude! And yet I
would have made you think you Made It all by yourself.
Behind every great man, as they said, there follows a
very surprised woman.

The thing is that most women are not even surprised!
If their child prospers, they did it. They cannot even
rejoice . . . unless they are there at the crowing
ceremony. I've seen more resentful Mrs. Elvsteds than I
have any wish to see again. For the faith in service has
gone . . . and the servants have learned too much about
their masters, and nothing you learn that way but has
its horrifying aspects.

"You'll learn, my girl", my mother says. "You'll learn."
And all she's doing is waiting for my father to retire,
when she will blossom and be strong enough for two.
"Take back your old rib, then, and use it for a crutch!"
I have hears my mother rehearsing it. I am just her
daughter; she does not pull any wool over my eyes. She
will go mad, my mother, when her time comes. No-one
should pride themselves on waiting and waiting and
never keeping anyone waiting themselves. The resentment that breeds is also the power to survive, for it is
necessary to see the one who thought you were dust
under their feet, lying helpless at yours.

"Take back your old rib, then, and use it as a crutch!"
How terrible to see so much hatred of the "thing" she
loved!

Oh I am rambling, Malcolm. And not to be believed.
My mother is envious of my freedom. I am afraid she
will realise that too.
I am unable to trust my mother to face the truth.
MALCOLM    The truth as you see it excludes charity.
FIONA    So I have to make my caricatures, my cartoon
poems. They are fiction. And lack authority.
MALCOLM    Wind us down. Or will I?
FIONA    I will not be like my mother. And yet I am
doomed to be . . . in some way.
MALCOLM    Your mother is easier to be with.
FIONA    Ah well, I'll be someone to put your feet up
with — eh? She has learned to be, in public, whatever is
wanted of her. She is never herself. Doesn't know what
that is.
(in an old woman's voice)    "Your father is mine. He
has taken no trouble to understand me. So he is
Mine.
And I am Nobody's!"
She actually was saying that, to herself in the mirror.
The power that comes from stored up resentments is a
diabolic power. I am afraid for her.
MALCOLM    Love her.
FIONA    God help us both, I do love her.
But she just judges me.
She will only love me if she's made me. If she can be,
what she calls "proud" of me.
MALCOLM    When she holds Virginia, she loves her.
FIONA    Oh Malcolm, that's it. Isn't it? That's it.
She is not responsible for Virginia, so she could maybe
love her just as she is.
MALCOLM    (changing mood)    I choose to see myself
as part of the revolutionary movement. I support talent.
Her talent. It is the manly thing to do. This is a philistine
society. They educate you here to become — guess what?

— a Bachelor! Eh? Or a Master! Implying of course a slave. And if they educate you a bit more, they dub you a Doctor! Such a society is obviously, selfconfessedly, Sick. There is no need to become apathetic, however. I have taken upon myself a Task. I have seen that my Task is Female. And Female is what Fiona is.

She isn't noticeably useful. My mother and her own can bake a better pie. And cartoon poems are a minority taste. Still, if I did not rally to her, Fiona would be expected to produce her "masterpieces" on the side, carrying the baby on her hip and her easel across her back. Hardly a free hand for the exercise of her craft. I'm not sure if she's any good at it. But the Need is there. She has something, and some of it's ugly alas, to say. But it does get it out of her system and too much long suffering is bad for the soul.

She gives performances at street corners or in Arcades. If I am not there to protect her, she excites fascist obscenities. If obscenities are required, she likes them to be her own. Large men — she says they all remind her of her father, whom she does not care for very much — he is not like me at all, and I can't say I am sorry she thinks that, because he is a man who is going much to seed and I am not. These large men tell her what they think she is really good for. (dirty laugh) And she is. Woman tell her to go on home and make me a good square meal. And she does, with tears salting the potatoes.

In public she is much too adventurous. She seems to me sometimes to have the deathwish of the desperate. Who could not pity her?

All she may be doing, of course, is reacting against her mother, who warmed the slippers for her dad, who never even said ta.

I, well, I find her an interesting subject.

FIONA    I    don't    really    know    what    I'm    about.

Sometimes I feel just part of a process. I can only hope that it's going forward.

MALCOLM    It was time I got married. It keeps the girl students off. And the boys too. I haven't the energy for homosexuality. People don't get sent to Reading Jail for it now, so one couldn't really embrace it as the courageous way.

Marriage seemed the answer.

It is heroism without the laurel wreath.

FIONA    Perhaps we could have a picnic.

MALCOLM    Here, in the Arcade?

FIONA    In Princes Street Gardens yesterday, it did not really alter anything.

MALCOLM    Of course other people were having picnics too.

FIONA    Even making love in front of John Knox while the queue waited for return tickets to Tartuffe — or was it The Bacchae — now there's diabolism for you — ugh — well, anyway our making love there didn't cause real comment.

MALCOLM    There was a counterattraction.

FIONA    Ian McKellan was slumming from Dr. Faustus at the Lyceum. I understand that in that play Helen just stands there and doesn't say a word. Talk about male fantasies!

MALCOLM    Ian McKellan knows people in the cast at the Assembly Hall, I suppose. That's really the only reason why a famous actor goes to see anyone else. For it must be really painful. But there was from the queue a wild rush for his autograph.

FIONA    I was really disappointed.

MALCOLM    Oh Fiona.

FIONA    No, I mean I was disappointed in them. They had their priorities wrong.

MALCOLM    People have very good manners. They

sort of looked away because they did not know us. Ian McKellan certainly looked away. But then he's from the South, the Metropolis most of the time I expect. They are more accustomed to that sort of thing there.

FIONA   We hoped they'd call a policeman. And cite John Knox as principal witness.

MALCOLM   Or pander.

MALCOLM   The policeman who eventually came was really rather embarrassed. You ought not to have smiled at him. He thought you looked so innocent. Because, no matter what, you really do!

Asked you if you wanted to prefer charges. Yet I don't really look like a rapist!

Or (preening himself) I don't know!

FIONA   I gave him a copy of my cartoon/poem — Variations on the Vagina.

MALCOLM   I recorded his reactions on mike. A sort of prolonged . . . Wha . . . hoo.

MALCOLM   It wasn't a profitless exercise. A fait accompli, I may say.

FIONA   Cock-a-doodle-do.

MALCOLM   Are we on the right lines, though?

FIONA   I sometimes wonder if what we are doing is silly. Perhaps all the battles are fought and won more . . . solemnly.

MALCOLM   All the battles are fought and . . . lost, Fiona . . . except if we begin with the personal ones. I may be here with my microphone to record the setting sun. But only the very solemn would let it go down without a whimper.

FIONA   You take the heart out of me.

MALCOLM   I am relying on you . . . girl.

FIONA   It will rise, the sun, tomorrow . . . and Virginia will enjoy it. Tell you what — I may even dare to give up a son . . . so long as you make me swear not to favour him particularly.

MALCOLM   I take it you don't want to manage that sort of thing alone. One does like a bit of . . . credit . . . occasionally.

(She runs to him and they embrace, I think.)